Plays by Karen Sunde

Broadway Play Publishing Inc
New York
BroadwayPlayPub.com

Plays by Karen Sunde
© Copyright 2001 Karen Sunde

All rights reserved. This work is fully protected under the copyright laws of the United States of America. No part of this publication may be photocopied, reproduced, stored in a retrieval system, or transmitted, in any form or by any means, electronic, mechanical, recording, or otherwise, without the prior permission of the publisher. Additional copies of this play are available from the publisher.

Written permission is required for live performance of any sort. This includes readings, cuttings, scenes, and excerpts. For amateur and stock performances, please contact Broadway Play Publishing Inc. For all other rights please contact the author c/o B P P I.

Cover photo: Peter Cunningham

First printing: June 2001
I S B N: 978-0-88145-192-4

Book design: Marie Donovan
Copy editing: Sue Gilad
Typeface: Palatino

CONTENTS

About the Author .... *iv*
Thanks .... *v*
Dedication .... *vi*
HOW HIS BRIDE CAME TO ABRAHAM 1
TRUTH TAKES A HOLIDAY 49
IN A KINGDOM BY THE SEA 103

ABOUT THE AUTHOR

Karen Sunde is an actor turned playwright. She performed some sixty roles Off-Broadway and was Associate Director of C S C Repertory. Plays of hers have been performed Off-Broadway, in regional theaters, on a U S A tour, and abroad—in ten countries and seven languages.

Sunde's first play, THE RUNNING OF THE DEER, was produced at C S C Repertory in New York in 1978. Her published plays are DARK LADY, produced at the Abbey Theatre, Ireland, and optioned for film; BALLOON, which won three *Villager* awards Off-Broadway, and was nominated Best Play by Outer Critics Circle (published by Broadway Play Publishing Inc); HAITI: A DREAM, produced at Seven Stages, Atlanta, and aired on W N Y C, W H Y Y, and N P R (published by B P P I in the collection FACING FORWARD); TO MOSCOW, premiered at Ankara National Theatre, Turkey and Chain Lightning in New York; and OH WILD WEST WIND. Scenes from TO MOSCOW; ANTON, HIMSELF; and MASHA, TOO appear in *Scenes & Monologs from the Best New Plays*. Her screenplay, *Deborah: The Adventures of a Soldier* was a finalist at Sundance.

For Actors Theater of Louisville; People's Light and Theater, Annenberg Center, Philadelphia; Wisdom Bridge, Chicago; and The Acting Company, New York, Sunde has written KABUKI OTHELLO, KABUKI MACBETH, KABUKI KING RICHARD and ACHILLES, which toured Hungary, Cyprus, and Japan. She co-wrote the musical QUASIMODO, which premiered at Byrdcliffe Festival, Woodstock, and ran a season at Lahti City Theatre, Finland. For Cheltenham Center for the Arts, Philadelphia, she wrote LA PUCELLE (ME & JOAN) and DADDY'S GONE A-HUNTING. Chain Lightning in New York originated and produced WHEN REAL LIFE BEGINS.

Sunde has completed screenplay *Parallel Loves* for Terra Bella Entertainment, and is writing *Dream House* for Passport Cinemas.

THANKS

Only TRUTH TAKES A HOLIDAY had a solitary birth. Both IN A KINGDOM BY THE SEA and HOW HIS BRIDE CAME TO ABRAHAM required midwives. My profound thanks to countless U N personnel and peacekeepers, to Brian Urquhart, Colonel Dermot Earley, Timur Goksel, Karen Van Arsdale, Naseer Aruri, Michael Dixon of Actors Theater of Louisville, Danny Fruchter of People's Light and Theater, Sonia Ragir, and Thomas Hoover.

DEDICATION

For all who serve

HOW HIS BRIDE CAME TO ABRAHAM

HOW HIS BRIDE CAME TO ABRAHAM had staged readings at Playwrights Theater of New Jersey, Madison, produced by John Pietrowski, which took place 25-26 September 1992 with the following cast and creative contributors:

ABRAHAM .... Adam Oliensis
SABRA .... Jan Leslie Harding
GRAMMA .... Joan Ludwig
DOG-STAR .... Jim Ligon

Director .... Cynthia Stokes
Production stage manager .... Steven Loehle

Further readings held at La Mama Galeria and Castillo in New York, and at Nebraska Repertory Theater

CHARACTERS & SETTING

ABE. *Young soldier, by nature tender, bright, coarsened by grueling duty.*
SABRA. *Young woman, ferocious, fine. Child's heart, locked in horrors.*
GRAMMA. *ABE's Gramma. Salty, warm as sunset, wise as time, old as can be*
DOG-STAR. *(Off-stage voice) ABE's platoon-mate. Rough, officious, human*

Note: Though ABE *and* SABRA *may be played by actors out their teens, an aura of innocence is essential.*

The set is a hillside, and a dugout field hut with its entrance hidden in the hillside. South Lebanon

(*House lights fade to black.*)
(*Explosion offstage. Then we hear soldiers' voices, off:*)

ABE: (*Off, terrified*) Benny!

DOG-STAR: (*Off*) What the hell...!

ABE: (*Off*) Help him!

DOG-STAR: (*Off*) Stop the blood.

ABE: (*Off*) Benny...! Move him out!!

DOG-STAR: (*Off*) Abe's hit too.

ABE: (*Off*) I'm all right. Leave me. Go!

DOG-STAR: (*Off*) Go!!

(*Dimly, lights come up on* GRAMMA, *perched unrealistically in the center of a rocky hillside, with undergrowth and grass, speaking warmly, intimately—*)

GRAMMA: The Lord is my shepherd, I shall not want....

(ABE *is calling now, from off.*)

ABE: (*Off*) Take it easy with Benny. Fast. Fast! Move!

(*Muffled moans and tramping through woods recede until only late afternoon sounds remain—birds, insects*)

GRAMMA: He maketh me to lie down in green pastures, he leadeth me beside the still waters, he restoreth my soul....

ABE: (*Dragging himself through grass at top of hill*) Stuff it, Gramma, I'm all right.

(ABE *pushes aside grass. He is badly wounded, close to delirium. She is content.*)

GRAMMA: Yea, though I walk through the valley of the shadow of death...

ABE: (*Shouts*) That's enough!

(GRAMMA *smiles, begins to hum an Israeli folk song.* ABE, *groaning with extreme pain, hoists himself into view to look around.*)

ABE: (*To himself*) God, Benny, God...why'd you stop here.

(ABE *is a very young Israeli Defense Forces [I D F] Corporal, by nature tender, but coarsened by his grueling recruit life.*)

(*He's breathing hard, from exertion while wounded, from shock, and to keep himself from crying. He's very frightened, his best friend has just been exploded, but he will handle himself like the man he has to be as long as he retains consciousness.*)

(ABE *twists, trying to note his surroundings, but sleep and shock are overcoming him.* GRAMMA *hums softly, blending with late afternoon sounds as he nods off.*)

(*Then, at sudden crackle from* ABE's *field radio, he snaps awake again. It could be, in fact, that the only "real" moments in the play are those when* ABE *hears the radio, and all else is the dream into which he escapes.*)

RADIO: Dog-star to Abe. Dog-star to Abe.

ABE: (*Dizzily*) ...What.

RADIO: Radio check.

ABE: (*Jerking awake*) Yeah. Yeah. You hear me?

RADIO: You're coming in clear.

ABE: (*Not wanting to know*) How's...Benny?

RADIO: He passed out. Just lost consciousness.

ABE: Get him the hell out of here!

RADIO: We'll send a squad for you.

ABE: Hell with me.

RADIO: You've gotta be in shock, Abe!

ABE: (*Dizzily*) First rest I've had since Basic.

RADIO: Don't fall asleep.

ABE: I'm in heaven.

RADIO: Abe, our procedures for this area don't allow...

ABE: Just get Benny out safe! I'm the leader. And fuck radio checks. I need a nap.

RADIO: Abe...!

(*He clicks off the radio, then painfully swings himself around, revealing a bloodied bare foot.*)

ABE: (*Responding to pain*) Fucking hell.

(*Blearily, he tries to look around him and listen. Then, deciding there's nothing to threaten him, he carefully places his foot and nods down in the grass again, to sleep.*)

GRAMMA: (*Intimate*) Thou preparest a table before me in the presence of mine enemies....

ABE: Yeah, yeah, Gramma, that's nice. But how 'bout you send me a Shabbat angel.

(GRAMMA *looks at him, smiles. He drops to sleep. She resumes humming, and gets up.*)

(Time or dimension change—lights drop swiftly, bird noises change to sunset, as GRAMMA *turns to watch upstage.)*

(Sudden cracking through brush, up left. ABE *sits up abruptly, wincing at his quick move, but fired with adrenaline, and holding his Galil automatic rifle at ready.)*

(More steps, a flutter of branches. ABE, *expecting an approach, conceals himself again, but his rifle barrel remains clearly aimed and poking out of the long grass.)*

(Pause. Then, the quiet patting of a slight, khaki-dressed Arab—head swathed in a plain kaffiyeh—coming onto upleft top of the hillside, and moving to upcenter)

*(*GRAMMA *looks at the Arab, and back towards* ABE, *smiling. Then she moves off, crossing the Arab on her way, handing the Arab a canteen, then continuing on off)*

(The rifle barrel moves, covering the Arab, who pauses, as after a long hike, unsuspecting, and takes a drink from the canteen.)

ABE: *(From the grass)* Halt.

(The Arab freezes, listening.)

ABE: Raise your hands, or I shoot.

(The Arab spins, diving toward ABE. ABE *fires, but the Arab is already on him. He swings the rifle barrel against the Arab's legs, tripping him, then rises onto his knees to grapple viciously, rolling with his prey to the edge of an upcenter ledge on the hill.)*

SABRA: *(Angry yell)* Aaahh!

ABE: Gotcha! You son of a bitch!

(They fight fiercely.)

(Finally, by crushing with his superior weight, ABE *controls the Arab, reaches to tear at the kaffiyeh, and is astonished when long dark hair tumbles out.)*

(Taking advantage of his surprise, the girl kicks him, wrenching away, and scrambling to her feet. ABE *howls from the blow to his foot, but re-aims his weapon from where he sits.)*

ABE: Stop! Or you're ground meat.

SABRA: Shoot me.

ABE: Come here.

(She stands glaring at him, panting.)

ABE: Come here!

(She moves slowly up to him.)

ABE: Give me your pack. *(Beat)* Give it! Slowly...

(She reluctantly slips off her knapsack, and lets it drop to the ground. As soon as she is within reach, he has hold of her hand, twisting it and her arm upwards, so she drops to her knees.)

ABE: Now sit.

(Not satisfied, he throws her forward onto her face.)

ABE: Get down!

(With his rifle jammed into her back, he dumps her pack. There's a map, an apple, which he eats immediately, and a white garment heavily embroidered in red.)

ABE: Where's your weapons?

(No response. He jabs with the rifle, she yelps, but won't respond.)

ABE: Where are they?

SABRA: You're the killer.

(He roughly and thoroughly frisks her for weapons.)

SABRA: *(Snarling)* Trespasser.

ABE: Yeah? And you're a fucking infiltrator.

SABRA: Sure.

(ABE has found a knife on her.)

ABE: What's this?

SABRA: For food, thief!

(Grabs her, shaking with his weak condition and frightened rage)

ABE: Benny's *blood* is draining all over your booby-trapped road. And you're fucking well going to pay!

(She spits at him.)

ABE: *(Grabbing her throat)* What are you doing here?

SABRA: *(Choking)* Get off my land!

ABE: Almost made it, didn't you? Only one more mile to the border. Where's your pals?

SABRA: Surrounding you.

(ABE pulls her roughly, close to him, like a shield.)

SABRA: Think I protect you? They'll shoot right through me.

(He twists her arm higher.)

SABRA: Aaaah!

ABE: Shut up!

(Silence. Both are panting heavily. ABE, on guard, expecting an attack, looks around.)

ABE: *(Long pause)* Maybe you are alone.

(She doesn't respond.)

ABE: Where are your weapons?

SABRA: What? My Kalashnikov? Grenade launcher? Pack of C 4? You think I've got nowhere to go? You think I'm a stinking *Palestinian*?

ABE: Who else.

SABRA: Ass among asses.

ABE: What are you doing here?

SABRA: Tending my land!

ABE: You're trying to cross the border. To murder Jews!

SABRA: How. With my fists?

(As she speaks she twists abruptly, flipping him away, and slides down the hill, tumbling to the stage floor. He yelps with the pain to his foot, scrambles, grabbing his rifle.)

(She flattens against the hillside. ABE, in extreme pain, is sliding down the slope, with one hand guiding him, the other holding his rifle poised. He lands, and covers her again with the rifle.)

SABRA: Hurt yourself?

ABE: *(Gasping, about to pass out)* Run. Go on!

SABRA: So you can shoot me?

ABE: *(Dizzy)* Why don't you run.

SABRA: Why should I. I'm home. *(She pulls vines aside to reveal a wooden door with iron fittings and lock, built into the hillside.)*

ABE: *(Startled)* Come here!

SABRA: Scared?

(She moves toward him. As soon as she is close enough he grabs her, and twists her in front of him as a shield, but he stumbles back with the pain, and they fall together, he clinging to her, but keeping the rifle trained on the door. They sprawl there, with him panting.)

ABE: Who's in there.

(She looks at him with almost a smile, taunting, refusing to answer.)

ABE: *(Jerking her roughly)* What is this? Where are we!

(They struggle again, futilely, until he stops, panting from exhaustion.)

SABRA: *(Pause)* Want the key?

ABE: Key... Who are you?

(She reaches into her shirt, and pulls a key from around her neck.)

SABRA: Or you'd rather blast it open. Purify it?

(He looks at her, not trusting.)

SABRA: Go ahead. Make it "pure." Kill everybody. Then you're safe.

(ABE *is unsure, his jaw grinds.*)

SABRA: 'Course if it's an ammunition dump...you fire, it explodes, and you've lost it.

ABE: *(Exhausted with pain, he snaps—)* Go.

SABRA: Go?

ABE: Slowly. To the door.

(*She eases away from him, approaches the door, glancing back at him. He covers her with the rifle.*)

SABRA: Now what.

ABE: Open it. Slowly. If you make a fast move...

SABRA: ...you'll fire. I know the game. (*She unlocks the door.*) Ready?

ABE: *(Pause, breathing hard, glaring at her, then—)* Open it.

(*She swings the door open, and stands aside, looking back at him. Nothing happens.*)

ABE: Move in front of it.

(*She steps to the center of the black opening, and looks at him. He doesn't know what to do.*)

SABRA: Well?

ABE: *(Frustrated)* Come back here.

(*She moves to him. Again, when she's near enough, he throws himself onto her, she staggers under the weight, but stays on her feet. He leans on her, shouting—*)

ABE: Well, move!

(*She moves with him attached, dragging him toward the door. As they go through it, the inside of the dugout is revealed by light coming up behind a scrim.*)

(GRAMMA *appears, speaks warmly, watching—*)

GRAMMA: Thy rod and thy staff, they comfort me....

(*The dugout is a field hut, crudely equipped for summer use, with old orchard tools, a wood stove, a pump, a few crates, gunny sacks.*)

GRAMMA: Thou anointest my head with oil, my cup runneth over.

ABE: *(As though dreaming)* I don't believe this. What is this place?

(SABRA *slides* ABE *off of her onto the one chair. Then she straightens, watching him in his bewilderment, then, without a word, she goes to the pump, pumps water into a pan, brings the pan, kneels in front of him, and lifts his bloodied foot onto her knees.*)

ABE: *(Involuntarily yelping)* Aaaaah!

SABRA: It's filthy.

(She begins bathing his foot. It is a gentle ritual. When outside, SABRA displayed all the cunning and ferocity of a trapped animal—one as frightened as he—but once through the door a calm graciousness pervades her actions. He doesn't resist, but watches her, breathing heavily, trying not to react to the pain.)

SABRA: Step on a land mine?

ABE: *(Grunting)* Damned P L O.

SABRA: It wasn't theirs.

ABE: What do you know about it.

SABRA: No P L O around here. You stepped on your own mine.

ABE: Fuck I did.

SABRA: And you're in shock.

ABE: It was P L O.

(She's reaching to get dirt from the deep center of the wound.)

SABRA: Have their name on it? You Israelis drop mines around like cow cakes.

ABE: *(Gasping from sudden pain of where she's hit)* Ahhh.

SABRA: *(Examining the spot)* Not at all pretty.

(Pause while he recovers himself, watching her work)

ABE: Why were you crossing the security zone?

SABRA: *(Incredulous)* Security?

ABE: You know what it's called.

SABRA: Security, yes—for Jews. On my land!

ABE: That's right!

(Stand off. They stare belligerently at each other.)

ABE: Why were you crossing it?

(She goes back to working on his foot, ignoring his question. But, finally—)

SABRA: Came for the apples.

ABE: Apples...?

SABRA: You've left me no brothers to do it.

(ABE stares at her, uncertain whether to believe her, or if so, what to answer.)

ABE: But, how did you....

SABRA: Get so far? Past your patrols, your snipers, your mines? This is Lebanon! You've no right to keep me out.

ABE: You must have....

SABRA: ...sneaked through. How else?

ABE: Why should I believe you?

SABRA: Because I felt safe, so you caught me.

ABE: I should believe you because I caught you?

SABRA: You never would have, not in a million years, if I hadn't felt safe. *(Finished bathing his foot, she drags a crate in front of him, and lifts the foot onto the crate.)*

SABRA: *(Lifting)* I'm at home.

ABE: *(Pained by sudden movement)* Aaahh!

SABRA: Keep it up there. Unless you want it the size of your head.

(SABRA carries the pan to the door, tosses bloody water out, goes back to draw water into a tin cup, and carries it to ABE.)

(He watches her in the submissive silence of his awkward and necessarily obedient position, then takes the cup, drinks thirstily without taking his eyes off her, then finally says whimsically—)

ABE: Did my gramma maybe send you?

SABRA: Who?

ABE: My gramma. I asked her to send me a Shabbat angel.

(She looks at him, but, without responding, moves away, fills the pan again, lugs a sack from the corner, sits on the floor with pan and sack. ABE, watching her every move, and examining the surroundings, tries another tack—)

ABE: This isn't your home.

SABRA: No? *(She takes a potato from the sack, examines and discards it.)*

ABE: No. No one lives here.

SABRA: You *let* no one. *(She roughly dumps out several potatoes onto the floor.)*

ABE: This is only a field hut. Where are you from?

(She looks at him, then returns to picking potatoes, dumping several into the pan of water. She will not respond.)

ABE: You said something about brothers. We'd left you no brothers?

(She doesn't look at him, but scrubs the potatoes ferociously. He watches her, his eyes flutter, wanting to close, and in that state, he remembers the explosion. The vision floods over him, and he's reliving it, like a bad dream.)

ABE: *(Murmuring)* Benny...

(He snaps awake, as though with a whiff of ammonia, and reaches for the radio, switching it on. It is his link with reality, but a reality so painful that he fears returning to it.)

(There's a static hum, and SABRA spins, on alert, like a fearful animal. ABE sees her, and they hold the look, like two animals surprised by each other in the woods.)

ABE: *(Pause)* I won't hurt you.

(SABRA *doesn't evade, but watches him warily, a potato in hand, but ready to run.* ABE, *shaken by the radio-hum's reality check, tries to reassure her.)*

ABE: I'm sorry about the...searching you. I know that in your culture... Well, we have orders not to even touch you. I mean, if you're a girl. *(Beat)* Not that I wouldn't like to... I mean, it seems years since I've even seen a girl, so... But I wouldn't have been so rough, if... *(Gasps, suddenly back in the explosion)* I...I saw the mine exploding, and Benny on top of it, and...God, his leg was....

(ABE *sees Benny with his leg blown off, then jerks himself out of the vision.)*

ABE: So I...I'm not quite...normal. And I...nothing seems real, you know? I mean, I'm still here. But who are you? Sitting beside me. And what are you doing? *(Little laugh)* Preparing the meal for Shabbat?

(The radio crackles, and SABRA *jumps, fearful.)*

SABRA: Someone's coming for you?

(An all-channels bulletin interrupts her.)

RADIO: Command to all channels. Headquarters under attack from unidentified P L O positions north. We're receiving heavy incoming mortar and R P G fire. Returning patrol squads proceed only under advisement. Repeat. Proceed to base only under advisement.

ABE: *(Sudden extreme fear, like unexpected tears—)* God! Did you get Benny through?

SABRA: *(Warily watching)* Someone's...coming for you?

ABE: *(Calming himself)* Probably.

(His attention is pulled back to her; he watches for a reponse, but she hides again in potato cleaning. Wearily, he lets the rifle slide and props it behind his shoulder.)

ABE: *(Casually)* 'Course they're coming.

(SABRA *is alert, stealthily watching him.)*

ABE: *(Trying to tease)* Think they'd leave me alone out here? With a stream of Jew-hating infiltrators?

(In one sudden move, she's up and bolting out the door. He clumsily twists to grab his rifle.)

ABE: *(Startled)* Wait! You can't...

(Three simultaneous actions: 1. ABE, *swinging his foot down, sways dizzily and collapses to floor.)*

ABE: Shit!

(2. SABRA, *at the same time, hesitates outside the door, considering whether to respond to his call, but instead, races toward the hill.)*

(3. At top of the hill, GRAMMA appears with an exploded, blood-covered boot.)

GRAMMA: I will fear no evil. The Lord of hosts shall lop the bough with terror, and Lebanon shall fall.

(GRAMMA places the boot prominently. SABRA is scrambling up the hill, ABE dragging himself across the floor to shelter beside the door.)

GRAMMA: *(Crouched behind boot, intimately)* Oh, inhabitants of Lebanon, how gracious shalt thou be when the pangs come upon thee...

(SABRA finds the boot, takes it in her hand.)

GRAMMA: *(Watching SABRA)* ...the pain as of a woman giving birth.

(SABRA looks back down the hill, and slowly, carrying the boot, descends, picking up firewood on her way.)

RADIO: Command to all channels. All combat ready units, report immediately.

(ABE is leaned, on alert for an attack, next to door. SABRA comes through door, meets his rifle barrel, which he holds on her an instant, then deflects, embarrassed, while she just looks at him.)

ABE: Welcome home.

(She moves straight across the hut, dumps firewood, and turns, holding bloodied remains of his boot towards him. It shocks him, but he bounces back on the next breath.)

ABE: How about that. My boot. Wherever I step, you'll make blood soup. Won't you.

(They look at each other.)

ABE: That's a joke. Like my gramma would say. *(Beat)* Not funny?

(She moves to him, crouches to let him lean across her, and drags him back to the chair.)

ABE: *(Gasping, as they move)* Aw...you're just pissed you can't get two good boots. Right? You'd trade for a Seiko diver's watch. Or a couple ounces of hash.

(She dumps him back onto the chair. He gazes up at her.)

ABE: What are you up to?

(She simply holds his boot out toward him. As he reaches for it, she notices something protruding from its torn lining. She takes hold, and draws out a flat piece of metal on a string.)

ABE: Extra dog-tags.

(She looks at him quizzically.)

ABE: In case you blow my head off. In case you want to know who my feet used to belong to.

(They hold their look for an instant, then she drops the tag in his lap and returns to her firewood.)

ABE: Not even curious? *(He picks up the tag, looks at it, reads.)* "Abraham Arik Mannheim. Corporal First Class. 9665379, Type O."

(He looks at her, but she's paying no attention, building a fire in the stove.)

ABE: Never know when it'll come in handy. *(Beat)* You don't think so? You don't want my dogtags? You could trade 'em for a dozen prisoners. We're crazy like that. We care about our people. *(Pause. He's getting angry.)* This is everyday business out here. Blood and corpses. You shouldn't be running lose!

(No response from her)

ABE: Listen. You don't want to be found out. You don't want to meet my buddies, right? You've been lucky so far. But I should have shot you on sight.

SABRA: *(Sudden, sharp)* Is that my fault?

ABE: Yes! You know this zone is forbidden.

SABRA: You have no *right* here!

ABE: *(Angry)* I'm talking reality, not rights. It's not my fault either, but I could have shot you. And that's just my orders. To protect *me!*

(He stops, glaring at her, but when she doesn't challenge, he calms down, watches her lighting fire.)

ABE: Sure you know how to do that?

(She glances at him, and goes on with her work.)

ABE: I mean, my sister wouldn't have the least idea...

(The fire catches. SABRA puts the pan over it, then turns, looking at him oddly.)

ABE: Yes. I have a sister. *(Now that he has her attention, he presses.)* Did you hear what I said?

(Ignoring the question, she steps toward him, and stands in front of him without speaking.)

ABE: What?

SABRA: *(Pause)* My knife.

ABE: *(Puzzled an instant, then—)* Oh. Sure. Sure.

(He reaches into a pocket, grunting with the pain of moving, retrieves her knife, then holds it, making her wait.)

ABE: Your eyes talk anyway. *(Beat)* At home Mama told me, "if you want something, use your mouth." But your eyes are talking. If I could just... translate. *(He hands her the knife.)* They look a hundred years deep.

(She looks at him, holding the utility knife in her hand. She opens it, still standing, looking at him. He refuses to be intimidated.)

ABE: *(Softly, with wonder)* What happened to you?

(Without speaking, she holds the look an instant longer, then suddenly moves back to the potatoes, and begins to slice them into the heating water. He watches, until he thinks he can catch her off guard.)

ABE: When you did talk, you lied.

(She glances at him, a bit startled.)

ABE: About what you're doing here. Doesn't figure. Too much risk. Your life for a few apples?

(She's uneasy, but doesn't respond.)

ABE: Got you, huh?

SABRA: Maybe it's...a gesture.

ABE: Sneaking in here?

SABRA: So the land won't forget me.

(She's motionless, speaking quietly. He watches her, trying to follow.)

SABRA: Just touching it. As though, if I don't visit, it'll be lost.

ABE: *(As still as she, moved)* You're beautiful now...naked. You're a child.

SABRA: *(Wanting to elude the intimacy, but caught)* What difference does that make.

ABE: But old enough to have a husband.

SABRA: A girl can choose. Whether to...

ABE: I thought it was "arranged" for her.

SABRA: In civilization it is. We live in disaster.

ABE: People still live.

(They look at each other, hold an instant, then suddenly, the radio crackles. Both jump.)

RADIO: Dog-star to Abe. Dog-star to Abe.

(She retreats, her focus frozen on the radio, as though it's a bomb. ABE watches her fright. For him, the radio is like a kick in his gut, and the horrifying reality of Benny sweeps back.)

ABE: *(Tense)* Abe here. How's Benny?

RADIO: *(Through static, evasive)* We...just got through. *(Beat)* The shelling's awful here.

ABE: I've got interference...what?

RADIO: I said the shelling....

ABE: How's Benny!

RADIO: We...we got him into emergency. He bled a lot, Abe, he....

ABE: What did the medics say!

RADIO: They're gonna see if they can sew him up.

ABE: *(Not believing it)* Sure.

RADIO: How are you doing?

ABE: *(Near tears)* Great. Great.

RADIO: You know we're under attack here.

ABE: I heard.

RADIO: Soon as it eases up, we'll find an A P C and be out after you.

ABE: I'll be here. Out.

(Radio clicks off. Drained, ABE looks at SABRA, gauging her fear.)

SABRA: They'll be coming.

ABE: They're under fire.

SABRA: But they'll be coming.

ABE: They're not coming yet.

SABRA: Then I'll go.

ABE: Go? You can't go.

SABRA: Yes. You'll let me.

ABE: *(Light, trying to tease)* Let you go? When I've got such a nurse-maid?

SABRA: Let me go.

ABE: You're free. You went for wood. You could run.

SABRA: You could shoot. And you have dogs.

ABE: Yeah.

(She looks at him, considering—will he fire?—then gathers her pack, eyes on him the whole time, and, still facing him, edges toward the door. She is going to run. But as she steps into the doorway, he points the rifle at her, and flips off the safety. She stops, caught.)

SABRA: You said I was free.

ABE: *(Beat)* But I'm not.

(She still stands poised to run. He doesn't back down.)

ABE: Are your potatoes boiling?

(She looks at the fire, but stays stubbornly in the door. He keeps the rifle on her.)

ABE: Why did you do all this?

SABRA: What.

ABE: Take care of me.

SABRA: *(Beat)* Arab hospitality.

ABE: For a Jew?

SABRA: *(Shrugs)* Anyone.

ABE: An invader?

SABRA: All right. I was lulling you. Till you fall asleep.

ABE: *(Smiling)* To see that, you'll have to stay.

(She huffs, frustrated, wanting with every ounce to be gone, holds there a beat longer, then flings down her pack, and moves back to the fire. ABE lowers the rifle, watches her a minute, then salutes her cheerfully.)

ABE: I'm Abe.

(She looks at him blankly.)

ABE: You have a name?

(She shakes her head.)

ABE: You don't?

SABRA: *(Pause)* You've taken it.

ABE: Your name?

SABRA: Who I am. Everything.

ABE: *(Lightly)* So you are my nameless captive. *(Beat)* Or I'm yours. I mean, you could kill me... *(Snaps his fingers)* ...like that. Being female, and clever, and all.

(She looks at him, makes no response.)

ABE: But maybe you don't want to make a mess.

SABRA: I want you gone.

ABE: Not simple.

SABRA: Just let me go back.

ABE: Back where?

SABRA: The way I came.

ABE: You're not that stupid! It's possible, just possible, if you're very careful where you step, to make it through these woods...in daylight. But at dark, they start to move.

(She is affected, watches him.)

ABE: And now it's dark. And now...a deadly stream comes slipping, probing, pouring through—all terrorists. You know that, don't you.

All ripe with blood lust. They don't care who they kill. Just so it's Jews. But we Jews are out here too. Every single night, in a new place, a new nest, we wait for them to come, we pick them off, they don't get through alive. *(Pause, as he stares at her)* So. You want to go out and take up sides?

(She meets his stare, but doesn't speak. He, angry at her stubbornness, is winding into a rage.)

ABE: We have machines that find you if you move. Or even if you don't. In daylight, I ask myself questions, a whole rule-book full, before I shoot you, but not at night. At night whatever moves is killed. *(Beat)* And it's getting worse. They're coming younger, they're coming loaded with explosives, they're coming on purpose to die! Kamakazis. Human bombs. You'd like to scoot out there and smack into one of them? Kids, with glassy eyes, looking to get to heaven?

SABRA: It's not heaven they want. You took their land.

ABE: You ready to join them? *(Pause)* Are you!?

(She won't answer.)

ABE: If you think you're safe out there, you must have friends I haven't met.

(She turns away.)

ABE: And what if the only reason your friends don't attack...is that I'm holding you?

SABRA: *(Derisive)* Tsaa.

ABE: Wrong?

SABRA: You'd be dead.

ABE: They'd sacrifice you to get at me?

SABRA: I'm alone!

ABE: *(Little smile)* Not...anymore.

(She shoots a look at him. He meets it, then smiles broadly.)

ABE: I'm hungry.

(Frustrated, she lets out a choked-off cry, but goes back to tending the potatoes. ABE watches her.)

ABE: *(Pause)* What are you afraid of?

SABRA: Nothing.

ABE: The other soldiers? Me?

SABRA: Nothing. *(Suddenly icy, direct)* There's nothing you can do... would make me afraid.

ABE: *(Pause)* Why did you bathe my foot?

(She looks at him without answering.)

ABE: Why?

SABRA: *(Pause)* It looked stupid.

ABE: Stupid? Hmh. Guess so.

(Unable to see in the late dusk, she gets a stick-end burning, brings a gas lantern from the wall, and lights it.)

ABE: Candles at sundown. Nice. *(Pause)* Want some flavoring...for your potato stew?

SABRA: What?

ABE: There's bully beef. In my bag.

(She looks at his bag, and back at him, swallows hungrily.)

ABE: It won't bite. It's de-horned.

(She moves, silent, to the bag, extracts the tin of beef, looks at him. He suddenly switches from teasing to quiet pleading.)

ABE: My silent Arab angel...we're only here because of the Palestinians. To keep them away from the border. The infiltrators. They're violating your country too.

(He puts out his hand for the tin. She hands it to him. He extracts a P-38 opener, and opens the tin. She's watching him steadily. He sniffs the can.)

ABE: Mmmh. Smell this.

(She ignores what he's saying, takes the tin, but continues to look at him without moving.)

SABRA: Just let me go.

ABE: You're afraid to face the soldiers.

SABRA: Don't you know what they'll do?

ABE: We'll have a great time together.

SABRA: *(Shocked)* What?

ABE: If you're who you say you are.

SABRA: They'll put me in prison. They'll destroy this place. They'll....

ABE: You think we're barbaric?

SABRA: I don't give it a name. I see what you do.

(He absorbs the sting of what she says, then sends back cold steel—)

ABE: *(Beat)* How much could you get for me? Live. From the P L O?

(She reacts with a hiss, and angrily moves back to dump the beef into the potatoes. Conversation over. Stony silence)

(He glances at the radio. Thinking of Benny but afraid to find out, he starts to reach for the radio, then looks back at her, remembering her fear, and decides to spare them both, by not calling in.)

(He continues watching her, sorry he cut off the talking. He adjusts the rifle, checking to see whether she's paying attention. She isn't. Finally he shifts, and yelps in pain. She looks his way, but doesn't respond. He moves again, gasping. She stops and looks at him. He sees he has her attention.)

ABE: I think.... Maybe it's drying too much. I...

SABRA: Have you got an undershirt?

ABE: What?

SABRA: An undershirt.

ABE: Yes.

SABRA: Take it off.

(He props himself, watching her quizzically, and unbuttons his shirt. She's moving with two plates of food. He waits with his eyes on her, to remove his undershirt when she can watch him. She puts the plates down beside him, then straightens, watching him. He takes off his undershirt.)

ABE: Well?

(She puts her hand out for the undershirt, takes it, and with quick jerks, tears it into broad strips. Then she goes to his kit without asking, searches in it, and brings out a tube of ointment, smears it lightly on his foot, then lifts and wraps the foot, gently. ABE bears all this in silence, his eyes on her every move, until—)

ABE: You're very...effective.

SABRA: *(Her eyes flash)* I've had practice. *(She continues wrapping.)*

ABE: You've done this before?

SABRA: More times than you dream of.

ABE: *(Quiet, earnest)* Tell me.

(She looks at him. Her face is open again; she wants to tell him, but the radio crackles. She jumps, but he puts out his hand, and makes the radio wait.)

ABE: *(Pause)* Are you sure...we're enemies?

RADIO: Dog-star to Abe. Dog-star to Abe.

(She looks at the radio, back at him, then moves away.)

ABE: Abe here. *(He breathes deep before asking.)* How's Benny.

RADIO: *(Beat, then, evading the question)* Can you verify your coordinates, Abe? We have you at 33.16 north, 35.32.5 east. That's roughly eleven kilometers from Beaufort Castle.

ABE: *(Trying to hold in his panic)* How's Benny?

RADIO: We're, uh, responding to incoming fire. We haven't been able to....

ABE: Answer me about Benny!

RADIO: He's out of surgery, Abe. But nobody can see him. It...doesn't look good.

ABE: Oh, god. Oh, god.

RADIO: Damn, Abe. Don't make me sorry I told you.

ABE: I'd have killed you if you didn't.

RADIO: Verify, Abe. Are those your coordinates. We've located an A P C. We're going to crash on through.

(ABE's *head is hanging, bent over the radio. Pause*)

RADIO: Abe? Do you read me? We're coming after you.

(ABE *slowly lifts his head, looks at* SABRA, *who's watching him like a cornered animal.*)

ABE: There's...no need.

RADIO: What?

ABE: Don't risk it. Not at night. I...found shelter.

RADIO: What shelter? Abe. Are you all right?

ABE: Just...start out in the morning.

RADIO: What about your foot?

ABE: *(Pause)* I washed it. *(Beat)* O K?

RADIO: Abe...I don't think....

ABE: I just need to keep it elevated. Out.

(ABE *clicks off the radio, sits still, breathing hard, wanting to push away the pain of Benny. He looks at* SABRA.)

ABE: Did you poison it? *(Reaches for his plate, watching her, smells it)* Uumm. Delectable poison.

(SABRA *stands looking at him.*)

ABE: Come. Sit by me. Eat.

(*She doesn't move, but continues looking at him.*)

ABE: Among Jews the women may now sit at table. Though not at prayer. Will you come?

SABRA: *(Not moving)* You didn't tell them.

ABE: Tell them what?

SABRA: About me. About this dangerous P L O infiltrator.

ABE: They might not sleep well, knowing.

SABRA: And you will?

ABE: *(Looks at her. Beat)* Is that a warning?

(For the first time, it seems, she smiles. Then, though still wary, she comes, takes up her plate, kneels near him on the floor to eat. ABE closes his eyes, says a blessing. She watches, then quickly, as he finishes, crosses herself.)

ABE: What's that?

SABRA: What.

ABE: You're not Muslim.

SABRA: Why do you ask.

ABE: You're Christian.

SABRA: What difference?

ABE: You crossed yourself.

SABRA: I'm Arab.

(He looks at her, puzzled. She begins eating, hungrily. ABE tries, but has little appetite. They continue throughout to watch each other. When she finishes, she's breathing hard from the fast eating. And still watching him. Pause)

SABRA: He's your friend.

ABE: Who?

SABRA: *(Beat)* Benny.

(ABE looks at her, surprised at her noticing, but then tight, bitter—)

ABE: Will it make a difference?

SABRA: A difference?

ABE: In whether you hope he dies?

SABRA: *(Pause)* Have you seen anyone die.

ABE: *(Startled, he holds her look, then lets spill—)* He's my best friend. We joined up together. He and my sister are... *(Breaks off, choked. Pause)*

SABRA: *(Soft, but noncommittal)* Death is easy.

ABE: He was teasing me, you know? We were on opposite sides of the road, plodding behind the Bedouin, the tracker, focused on the ditch, for anything—wires, barrels, trash—anything signifying "bomb here." But Benny stops... Telling me he's spotted a yellow-bill. He's such a goof. He won't believe in danger. And we have this standing bet—whoever spots a yellow...

   He must've been standing on the thing already, right on it. And I got close, knocked into him, deflected him just a bit, and.... It was so loud. Then, just a ringing sound, like my ear drum had snapped, before I remember him slipping down next to me, his guts a mess, and his leg... gone. Oh, God. *(Doubles over, can't say more)*

SABRA: *(Pause)* It might've been worse.

ABE: What?

SABRA: If you hadn't taken...part of the force of it.

ABE: You know what a blast does to flesh? The way it flings everything, bursts, just like a... *(Moans, as though sick, then looks at her, and realizes)* You do know. You know everything, don't you?

(He takes her hand. She looks at him, startled, unsure, then attempts to withdraw her hand, but unsuccessfully.)

ABE: Don't...move. Don't be afraid. What can I do? I can't run after you.

(She sits still, watching him warily.)

ABE: What does this do? Does this compromise you? Are you defiled if I hold your hand? What's going to happen here? O K. You want me to let you go? Tell me who you are.

(He waits. She doesn't respond.)

ABE: It's easy. "Abe, my name is Nadia. I come from..." Wrong? Is your name not Nadia?

SABRA: *(Pause)* Sabra.

ABE: Sabra? That's not a name. Is it? Sabra? All right, all right, it's a start. You're Sabra. And you can't live here now, but you live...where? Beirut?

(He looks in her eyes, and she looks at him, but doesn't answer.)

ABE: That's it? You've come all the way from Beirut? Why won't you tell me?

(First she just shakes her head slowly, then finally says, calmly—)

SABRA: I don't exist.

ABE: You don't exist. You're some...spirit of the woods. I'm imagining you?

SABRA: *(Pause)* Maybe you are.

ABE: Well. Something brought you here. There's some reason you're "visiting" me.

SABRA: No...

ABE: No?

SABRA: Why are you here?

ABE: Me? Dumb luck.

SABRA: Luck?

ABE: Sooner or later, it runs out. That's what they tell you.

SABRA: Runs out.

ABE: And that's when you step on a mine. Whammo.

(The joke he was making turns on him; the "whammo" becomes Benny being blown up. He lets out a contorted cry, but comes out of it gasping, having found a reason it happened—)

ABE: Aaaah! It's because Benny was 'short'—only four days till he'd go home—that's when you let down, when you dream you're out of it, next step to being free—and he pulled me along into his dreaming, just like... God. This whole thing is fatal. I can believe you don't exist. And you conjured this place, just to trip my reflex—"Let go. You're safe home."

I'm out here forty days at a time, and every minute of every hour of those forty, I keep a vision of my death, moving with me, clear. I have to. Because I'll never see my waiting death...before it comes. And I have to stay alive. So my eyes are dry, on constant alert, sweeping, with my head swiveling after, sprung off my taut neck. "Don't blink. Don't let down. Catch anything that moves."

But on a warm summer night...it's impossible. Spread out for ambush, lying in the grass, impossible. It gets so clear, so soft. The star fires so close overhead. How can I keep death alive...inside me?

(ABE stops. SABRA's watching attentively. She looks at her, holds a moment, then, as though embarrassed at revealing himself, asks abruptly—)

ABE: What do your parents say about you?

SABRA: *(Averting her gaze)* My parents.

ABE: Yes. Is this—what you're up to—proper behavior for a fine young Arab of good...

(He stops himself, seeing she's upset.)

SABRA: *(Matter of factly)* I don't have any.

ABE: No parents?

SABRA: *(Looks at him)* It was a bomb. In a car.

ABE: And that's why you don't exist?

SABRA: *(Shakes her head, vaguely)* No. I never existed.

ABE: Sabra. Your brothers. You said....

SABRA: They weren't really my brothers. They're Um Sa'ad's sons.

ABE: *(Glad to have an answer he can translate)* Um Sa'ad. The mother of Sa'ad. She...raised you?

(SABRA looks at him with quiet eyes.)

ABE: *(Satisfied to finally have a clear answer)* Well. That's something.

SABRA: How many Arabs have you killed?

ABE: None. None! Sabra, listen. I asked for this. I transferred here, out of Israel, so I wouldn't wind up killing children! I don't like this. You think I want to kill someone? I don't hate Arabs. I only want to live in peace. But they keep on coming to kill us.

And I'll tell you, it's not like you think. They've got no chance here. No chance to win. To even fight. I've seen it work. One night on ambush, I crawled back to the APC, the tank, and inside, they're watching with a night-scope, on a screen, like a video cartoon! And there come the stick creatures. They show up on the screen because they're alive out there, they're warm, they're moving—not even close, a whole kilometer away! And because it's night, we don't ask—we just fire. We fire, several rounds, and every shell seeks warmth, and bursts itself in flesh. We watch. In silence...the creatures falter on the screen. No shrieks. Nothing. The stick shapes just begin to fade, getting dimmer as their warmth is lost, until they blank out, blending with the screen, completely cold. *(Pause)* No. I've never *seen* anyone die.

SABRA: *(Darkly)* Lucky.

ABE: *(Shouts)* I'm protecting the border, farmers two kilometers from here! Am I allowed to defend my home?!

(His outburst strikes her strangely. She looks at him, open, like a child.)

SABRA: *(Quiet)* Home. Yes. *(Pause)* What's it like.

ABE: I... What?

SABRA: Your home.

ABE: *My* home.

SABRA: Yes. You have one?

ABE: Of course!

SABRA: What's it like.

ABE: It's.... What do you mean?

SABRA: A house. A farm?

ABE: Just a house. A...

SABRA: On a hill?

ABE: Well... Yes, a hill.

SABRA: Is there a tree?

ABE: What are you after?

SABRA: It's old, isn't it.

ABE: *(Amused)* I don't understand.

SABRA: *(Asking him to imagine himself there)* You're at home. You see your mother. Your father. A rug by the door. A picture of your sister and you—but younger.

ABE: *(Seeing his home)* Yes...

SABRA: Are you afraid?

ABE: At home? No.

SABRA: No one is?

ABE: My gramma.

SABRA: She's afraid?

ABE: My mother was born in a camp...in Germany.

SABRA: A camp? With no sewer.

ABE: No, I think...I think they had a sewer.

SABRA: She was afraid.

ABE: Yes. Sometimes she still is.

SABRA: But, then, in the camp with her baby—your gramma had no home.

ABE: No, then she didn't. And later...

SABRA: Did someone take it? Did she fight?

ABE: Not... It wasn't exactly....

SABRA: You have to fight. It's your home.

ABE: Yes.

SABRA: If they come in the night. Where it's safe. Where your mother holds you. Where you go to sleep.

ABE: *(Alarmed)* Sabra. What is it? What happened?

(She stops, looks at him, her eyes soft and hurting.)

ABE: How old were you.

SABRA: How old?

ABE: When your parents were killed.

SABRA: Old. Plenty old.

ABE: How many years?

SABRA: *(Pause. Without emotion)* Eight.

(ABE swallows hard, and, not knowing what to say, covers his readiness to cry with whimsy, wanting to make her smile.)

ABE: And here you are...apple hunting—a spirit in the woods, who's snatched me, this unsuspecting soldier, a spirit...who doesn't even exist.

(She only looks at him.)

ABE: Does Um Sa'ad tell stories?

SABRA: Stories?

ABE: Yes. Good stories.

SABRA: Not...now.

ABE: But before.

SABRA: Sometimes. About a bird.

ABE: Tell me.

(She looks far away.)

ABE: Don't go.

SABRA: I'm not.

ABE: Yes, you did. You raised your wings.

SABRA: No.

ABE: You left. You tried.

(She looks at him.)

ABE: You're my captive here. You have to stay in my good graces. I want to see this hand. *(He takes her hand, turns it to look at her palm.)* Aha. You know what I see here? In this line here. *(Tracing it)* This life line...

SABRA: I don't have any.

ABE: Ah ah ah, let me look. What I see is a good hand, a strong one. It... it dreams. It feels...many things. It needs to build a strong life. I have hold of it here, you see? It does...exist.

(She looks at him. Her mouth opens, but no sound comes out. Then, suddenly, she weeps, hard, bends over weeping. He is startled, nearly weeps himself. He puts his arm around her. She sobs, clings to his arm.)

ABE: Don't. Don't, don't, Sabra. It's all right.

(He leans over, kisses her hair. Then kisses her cheek. She breathes deep, catching her breath, realizes what's happening, raises her head to look in his face, questioningly.)

ABE: I'm sorry. I...

(He stops speaking, goes on looking at her as she gazes at him. Then, suddenly, she leans forward and kisses him on the mouth, slowly, then pulls back again to look at him. He smiles.)

ABE: Well. Thank you. That...I'm sure that did happen.

(She leans forward again, and kisses him a bit longer, and pulls back again to look at him. She reaches her hand to touch his face, curiously. Watching her, silent, he takes her hand from his face, and kisses it, several times, all over, still watching her. She leans forward again, and, instantly they are holding and kissing each other.)

ABE: Don't hurt, don't hurt, please don't hurt so much.

(They go on kissing until she pulls back, catching a breath.)

SABRA: I'm your enemy.

ABE: Yes. Yes, you are. *(Kisses her gently)*

SABRA: Why did you come here?

ABE: To be with you.

(They kiss again until she suddenly puts her hand over his mouth, and averts her head to listen, alarmed.)

SABRA: Shhhh. *(Douses lantern, listening, then darts to door, cracks it open, listens)* It may be nothing. *(Pause. Listening again)* If it's your soldiers...

ABE: They'd warn me first. How about yours? More, uh, apple farmers?

(She shoots a look at him, but doesn't answer the challenge.)

ABE: For all I know, we're sitting on the main road to the promised land.

SABRA: What would happen to you if...

ABE: *(Pause)* If what.

SABRA: What would your Captain say? About me.

ABE: If he found me with you? Dumb luck.

(She turns away to the door.)

ABE: I'm teasing, Sabra. Come here.

SABRA: It's dark.

ABE: Yes. It's dark now. No one can find us. Come here.

(She stands watching him.)

ABE: Yes. You're right. I'd be in giant trouble. Even for talking, let alone... touching.

(She moves slowly back to sit beside him.)

ABE: So, my Shabbat angel, tell me your story.

(She looks away.)

ABE: This is not fair, you know. I don't even know your name.

(She looks at him.)

ABE: Sabra isn't your name.

SABRA: Abraham.

ABE: That's mine.

SABRA: Abraham.

ABE: How about your "brother," Sa'ad?

SABRA: Yes.

ABE: Um Sa'ad's first born. What happened to him?

SABRA: He went to the fighting. She wanted him to be a priest. But he went to the fight.

ABE: What fight?

(She looks at him, and away.)

ABE: Against Israelis? He's with one of the factions?

SABRA: No more. Shot through the throat. *(Pause)* She says she gives them. It's all she can do. She gives sons.

ABE: And the other?

SABRA: Hamid.

ABE: Hamid.

SABRA: He'd curl my hair round his finger.

ABE: Hamid is....

(She bites her lip, turns away.)

ABE: Tell me.

SABRA: Hamid studied to doctor. He didn't believe in the fighting.

ABE: Then what.

SABRA: *(Simply, without emotion)* Your soldiers took him anyway. They must have thought he knew...would tell...about his brother. So they...they tried to make him. They beat him every day, they beat him on the head until... his eye was crushed, and then, so no more marks would show, they hanged him naked by his wrists. *(Beat)* They piped in screeching, screams of others, and wouldn't let him sleep. They made him crawl and bark.

ABE: *(Feeling the story too horrible)* No...please...

SABRA: They cut his feet. They...

ABE: Stop, please...

SABRA: ...did things...to his sex, it was...

ABE: That's enough.

SABRA: *(Pause)* He didn't ever sign their paper. But when they let him out, before he died he told Um Sa'ad—they were so strong, they must be right, he wished...he were a Jew.

(ABE's head goes back, mouth open without a sound, then drops forward, weeping. SABRA looks at him.)

ABE: I can't...believe this, Sabra. When was this.

SABRA: *(Dry)* He came home blind. Then he died. That I saw.

(Breathing deep, ABE calms himself, then looks at her, determined to go on.)

ABE: Before. When you were only eight...did you have real brothers or sisters?

(SABRA gets up swiftly to move away, but he holds her hand to stop her.)

ABE: Sabra:

(She stands silent.)

ABE: I'll stop asking. Sit with me.

(She stays standing.)

ABE: Don't be...please don't...be afraid of me.

SABRA: *(Softly, a vow)* Your name shall be Abraham...for a father of many nations have I made thee.

ABE: Yes. That's what they say. *(Little laugh)* And I try to understand it.

SABRA: *(Gaining strength)* And the angel of the Lord called unto him out of heaven, saying "Abraham. Abraham." And he said "Here I am."

(She slowly extends her hand to him, and he takes it, carefully.)

SABRA: Where do you come from, Abraham?

ABE: Jerusalem.

(Startled, she seems to breathe a cry of joy.)

SABRA: No...!

ABE: I do. Have you seen it?

SABRA: *(Her mouth opens, but for an instant, she doesn't speak, then—)* No.

ABE: But everyone knows...

SABRA: Yes. Everyone knows Jerusalem.

ABE: You have to come. You have to see it. The great mosque is brilliant, so...breathtaking, cut out of the blue sky.

SABRA: *(Shyly)* And the air...rings?

ABE: *(He laughs.)* It does! It's so clear.

SABRA: *(Slowly smiling. A glow begins to warm her.)* Everyone comes from Jerusalem.

ABE: Yes. When you're there, you know. All...all of Abraham's children.

(He's troubled, and feels like weeping, so he smiles and reaches for her. But she holds back, wanting to tell him something.)

SABRA: *(An excitement beginning)* This night...is like no other.

ABE: *(Small laugh)* That's for sure.

SABRA: You don't understand, but...you will. I...

ABE: You can tell me.

(She shakes her head, unable to go on. He just wants her close to him.)

ABE: Then come. Tell me the bird story.

SABRA: What story?

ABE: About the bird.

SABRA: That Um Sa'ad tells?

ABE: Yes.

SABRA: It just learns to fly.

ABE: *(Smiling)* That's all?

(As she begins, ABE draws her until she's sitting close to him. She tells it like a child.)

SABRA: The bird is born in a terrible desert, ugly and full of screams.

But the bird has a dream of an olive tree, and awakes thinking she's lost, because the dream—an old stone wall with eggplants growing, and strawberries along its foot, and at its end, a silver, rustling, olive tree— is filling her mind, until she believes that this is real, and the ugly iron desert full of terrible cries is the dream.

So she tells herself "If you could only fly, you could lift out of this dream and find the sweet, warm, real world." And she begins to try. First she just runs. And runs, and runs, along the sharp edge, flapping her flimsy wings, until she begins to feel a bit of strength seeping across her back and out toward the pinions. Then one day, when she runs and flaps until she feels almost dizzy, she forgets to stop and keeps on flapping out past the edge and into the sky. *(She stops, and sits silent.)*

ABE: Does she find it?

SABRA: What.

ABE: The dream.

SABRA: Which dream?

ABE: The one with the olive tree.

SABRA: No, it's real.

ABE: Does she find it?

SABRA: I don't know.

ABE: You don't?

SABRA: I always fall asleep in the clouds.

ABE: Ahhh.

(She smiles suddenly, like sun coming out, then looks at him, shyly.)

SABRA: Are you married, Abraham?

ABE: Me?

SABRA: Are you married?

ABE: *(Laughing)* No.

SABRA: Good.

ABE: Yes. That's lucky.

SABRA: But you are...a man.

ABE: What?

(She doesn't repeat the question, but averts her eyes.)

ABE: Am I a man?

(Realizing she means sexually)

ABE: Well, yes. Yes.

SABRA: *(Quiet)* Good. *(Beat)* Because I'm going to love you.

ABE: What.

(She looks at him an instant, then rises, gets a quilt, and spreads it on the floor in front of him. He watches, not able to believe he heard right.)

ABE: Sabra...

SABRA: *(On her knees, looking at him)* Come.

ABE: I don't...

SABRA: You don't what?

ABE: I don't know what....

SABRA: But will you be happy?

ABE: When?

SABRA: When I love you?

ABE: Yes! But Sabra...

SABRA: *(Rising to let him lean on her)* Then come.

(She puts her arm around him, and lifts. He, rises, then slides as she lowers him, gently, onto the quilt. She makes him comfortable, may loosen his clothing.)

ABE: You're teasing me. You aren't serious.

SABRA: Oh yes. Very serious. This night is important to me, Abraham. I don't expect you to understand.

ABE: *(Ironic)* Oh, I understand how important this is. That's why....

SABRA: Don't you want me, Abraham?

ABE: Yes! Yes, I do.

SABRA: Good.

ABE: But have you...?

SABRA: Have I what?

ABE: Have you...loved someone before?

(She stops, smiles warmly at him, and speaks emphatically, as though she's taking a vow.)

SABRA: No, Abraham.

(He, astonished, perplexed, stares at her.)

ABE: Well then, you can't!

SABRA: No? *(Kneeling beside him, with one little shy intake of breath, she begins to unbutton her shirt.)*

ABE: *(Whispers)* No... *(Shouts)* Sabra, stop it!

SABRA: Don't be afraid, Abraham.

ABE: Sabra...

SABRA: *(Reaching to touch him, reassuringly)* You came to me from Jerusalem.

ABE: But your father...your brothers... You have uncles?

(She kisses him. She undoes her pants, pulls them off, kneels in her underpants.)

ABE: Sabra, you know better. They'll kill you.

SABRA: Shhhh. It won't hurt your foot.

(He pulls her to him, kisses her breasts. She watches him, touching his hair, then embraces him, kisses him, and bends to unbutton his pants.)

ABE: Sabra, we can't.

SABRA: Yes. Yes, we can.

ABE: A woman who shames her family...can be killed.

SABRA: It's no shame. No shame.

ABE: Listen to me.

SABRA: You lie, Abraham. You're ready. You want to come into me.

(She leans to kiss him. He pulls her on top of him.)

ABE: Oh my god.

SABRA: If I promise you. I promise you, no one will know. Never, never know.

ABE: Sabra...

SABRA: You want me. Help me. Show me how. It's just once. Do you want me?

(They kiss hungrily, until he stops, and sits up abruptly.)

ABE: What makes you think I know how?

SABRA: *(Sits up with startled cry—)* Abraham!

ABE: *(Ready to be defensive)* What?

SABRA: You don't? You've never loved someone?

ABE: No, I haven't! But that's not what matters here.

SABRA: Yes, yes, it does. It's perfect!

ABE: *(Pulling her down into his arms)* Please, Sabra, we have to stop.

(But they go on, neither wanting or trying to stop.)

SABRA: It can't hurt me, Abraham. It's life. Just once, I want life.

(Lights fade to nearly black.)

(In the dark, SABRA slides to lying beside ABE. Pause. Night sounds. Then, ABE, hearing something, starts slightly, rises onto an elbow. We hear humming, the Israeli folk song.)

ABE: *(Groggy)* What?

(GRAMMA enters, and, speaking to him, though not seen by him, moves toward him, and settles lightly just above his head.)

GRAMMA: *(Intimate)* Never mind, Abraham, I know what you want to tell me.

ABE: Oooh. Gramma.

GRAMMA: But a boxcar, Abraham, slamming shut. That's the thing I remember. That sound. The dark. I'll never forget. With your grandfather still outside. And your mother kicking me from inside...oh, Abraham. And the hell, the bottomless...hell that was coming, I didn't imagine, but I knew... that slam was the end of life. But you know, Abraham, after all...it wasn't.

(She reaches, gently pats SABRA's hair, then rises, and moves off, humming. ABE and SABRA sleep.)

(Dim streak of light, not yet dawn. SABRA raises her head. The two are entwined. Abe half-wakes, holding her, but she murmurs to him—)

SABRA: It's nothing. I have to go behind a bush. Sleep, my Abraham.

(He lets her slide away from him. She goes to the door, opens it, looks back at ABE, sees he's sleeping. Then she creeps to center, lifts a floor board, reaches down, and extracts a belt, which she straps to herself, then small rectangular packets the size of cigarette packs, which she places in pockets of the belt, and a small unit that resembles a radio, with wires. She looks back at ABE, pulls on her pants, buttons her shirt. He turns, groans.)

(She hovers to assure him, then drops to the floor to extract a revolver and rounds, closes the floor board, pick up her shoes and her pack, then moves out the door.

While outside, she pulls on her shoes, and loads the revolver. Inside, ABE *rolls over swiftly and sits up, listening. With revolver in hand,* SABRA *moves back to the door.* ABE *hears her coming and lies back down as though asleep.* SABRA *enters, approaches him quietly, stands over him, with the revolver poised. He is still. Suddenly, as she turns to leave, he rolls, and tackles her. The gun flies out of her hand.)*

ABE: Delilah!

SABRA: *(Struggling)* No!

ABE: *(Howls)* Delilah!

SABRA: Let go! You'll get hurt!

ABE: *I'll* get hurt. You thieving bitch! You sneaking, poisonous bitch! Why should I let you go? So you can reach your gun?

(He's pinned her with his weight, now bends her arm. She cries out in pain.)

SABRA: Ahaaah!

ABE: You're P L O.

SABRA: No...

ABE: Shut up! You are! And I'm a first-rate Jew-guilt sap. What a joke. Hilarious.

SABRA: Abraham...

ABE: Don't talk to me. Don't you *dare* use my name. Bitch!

SABRA: I have to go.

ABE: Sure you do.

SABRA: I have to go before your soldiers come.

ABE: Why didn't you slice my gut open? Why didn't you cut out my heart?

SABRA: Yes! Why didn't I?

ABE: *(Stopped. Beat, then realizes)* Because you've got a bigger plan. Not just to butcher me. You've planted a bomb. *(Beat)* I saw you, witch!

(He looks at her, eases up, finds he can hobble, with pain, but without passing out. SABRA's *eyeing him now, frightened. He glares at her.)*

ABE: Where?

(She won't respond. He pulls up on her arm. She yells.)

SABRA: Ahaa!

ABE: Where is it?

(She doesn't answer.)

ABE: You figured you'd get us all at once. Where did you put it, bitch!

(He yanks her arm again. She yells, then gasps.)

ABE: You think I won't break it?

SABRA: *(Gasping)* You think I'll tell?

ABE: Of course not. Come on.

(He lurches to the doorway, leaning on her, with her arm locked. She screams with pain.)

SABRA: Abraham, I told you...

ABE: ...lies! Lots of lies. *(Beat)* Here. By the door? So when it shuts we get it in the face? Kaboom! Oh, baby, you should have blown me away when you had the chance. Because you've got another load set to rip my buddy's guts out, and nothing, nothing is a bloody enough way to settle with you!

(He's jerking her around with him, trying to find wires or a telltale sign of a fresh mine planted.)

ABE: Stick with me, 'cause if it finds us before you give me the word, you're going with me...all the way, baby. *(As he pulls her)* Why the hell did you have to hit on me! What kind of sickness was that? Answer me!! *(Yanking her arm)*

SABRA: Ahhahhh!

(He lets loose, she's gasping, her strength gone, sliding down. ABE, gasping himself, and collapsing from pain, braces himself up off the ground, suddenly realizing—)

ABE: You did it, didn't you. You planted the shit that hit Benny.

(Still breathing hard, she looks at him.)

ABE: Didn't you?!

SABRA: *(Pause. Her eyes on him)* You won't believe me. So believe what you want.

ABE: You bitch...

SABRA: I told you....

ABE: You told me lies!

SABRA: I told you everything I could. You'll understand after....

ABE: After what?!

SABRA: There's nothing to find. You have to let me go.

ABE: I saw you with the stuff!

(He grabs her body round the middle, struggling to lift her, and feels the bulk of her belt, just as she swings her leg, ramming hard into his injured foot. He's thrown backwards, howling. She scrambles inside the hut for her gun, and picks up his rifle, covering him with it.)

SABRA: Stay there.

(ABE struggles to his feet. He stands frozen, astonished, staring at her.)

ABE: *(Pause, then finally—)* It's on you. I felt it.

SABRA: *(Breathing hard)* Come back inside, Abraham.

ABE: *(Not moving)* The stuff is on you. You're the bomb.

SABRA: Come in. Sit down.

ABE: Why. *(Pause. Not moving)* Why?

SABRA: I don't want to hurt you.

ABE: Hah! *(Beat)* What are you doing, Sabra?

SABRA: Nothing that concerns you.

ABE: No?

SABRA: No.

ABE: You're just going to blow yourself up.

SABRA: Maybe.

ABE: Maybe? When do you decide?

SABRA: I don't.

ABE: You don't! You just hop on down to the border and wait for somebody to shoot you? Or watch for a school bus to ram yourself into? Or what!

SABRA: You'd better go in now. Standing out here isn't good for you.

ABE: Sure. Sure.

(He spits, lurches back through the door, and flings himself into the chair. She follows, watching him.)

ABE: So what are you going to do with your jackass? Or should I say, your stud.

(She stands looking at him.)

ABE: You lied to me.

SABRA: Some.

ABE: You're Palestinian.

SABRA: I come from Jerusalem.

ABE: My god. *(Beat)* Palestinian.

SABRA: *(Quietly)* I'm going home.

ABE: Dressed like that?

(She moves to the radio.)

ABE: That's what was wrong with your story of Hamid. I should have picked it up.

SABRA: *(Swift, animal attack)* It makes sense now? What you did to him? Now that you know he was Palestinian?

ABE: *(Icy)* When were you ever in Jerusalem.

(She turns to him, shakes her head, unable to speak.)

ABE: When?!

SABRA: *(Hoarsely)* Never.

ABE: *(Triumphant)* Never.

(Pause. She walks close to him, brings her face close to his, and, shaking her head, whispers—)

SABRA: Never.

ABE: *(Understanding her)* Sabra...

SABRA: *(Stepping back, the gun still trained on him)* I know there were oranges there. On the hill. My father was six. In the night Jew soldiers came, firing shots, shouting loud "Get out!" His eyes opened wide—the first time he ever saw soldiers. "Get out, or we'll kill you!"

His father had no gun. "I can't leave my garden, my trees!" My father held his little dove, close, under his shirt. A soldier took his mother by the hair, and dragged her. They were all shoved out onto the road, with guns, where hundreds of families were running, as though from fire. "Please, let us go back for the stove, for the trunk, for some bread!" There were old who barely could walk, babies clinging to sleeves. "Keep moving!"

The third day his mother stumbled, and didn't get up. They dug a hole by the road. The dove was lost before that.

ABE: *(Pause)* That's a story.

SABRA: Mine.

ABE: A war story.

SABRA: What war? My family was just living!

ABE: I've got stories, too, Sabra. Want to hear them? Stories like this are passed down and down....

SABRA: This one you should understand....

ABE: ...and *changed.*

SABRA: ...if your grandmother lost her...

ABE: *(Enraged)* Don't you dare!! My grandmother has nothing to do with you.

SABRA: *(Stepping away, quietly)* "Wait just till the fighting stops." his father said. But when it did, and they started home... The border was shut. With machine guns. They took his father for "questioning." The family waited. He didn't return. *(Pause)* I was born in Sabra.

ABE: *(Startled, uneasy)* The camp?

SABRA: The camp. *(Pause)* My father couldn't forget his father's oranges. He went to fight his way back. When I was eight, Israelis came to Sabra. They surrounded the camp with their tanks. They sent in soldiers....

ABE: *(Sharp)* Not Israeli soldiers!

SABRA: No.

ABE: Not Jews!

SABRA: You don't want to hear this story?

ABE: Why don't you kill me? You've come to kill people.

SABRA: Jews.

ABE: People with children.

SABRA: And oranges. People with homes. But who? The Jews who stole my grandfather's orchard, the ones who made Hamid blind, the ones who stood outside the fence while my mother was....

ABE: I'm a Jew. And they aren't me!

SABRA: But you're the only one I know.

ABE: So kill me! *(Pause)* You can't.

SABRA: Yes I can. *(Beat)* I kept thinking of ways.

ABE: Does your God enjoy killing?!

SABRA: Does yours?

ABE: *(Almost laughing)* Oh, you'll be welcome in Jerusalem. Center of the world, city of God, the first God ever to say "you must not kill." Where everyone says they come to worship, but what they do there is hate. The city stinks of blood. *(Pause)* They'll tell you there's another Jerusalem. A pure one, hanging above the first one in the sky. It's a lie. There's only one. But why can't its golden light burn off its poison! *(He looks at her, exhausted, and as bitter sarcasm surges, he goes on, fiercely—)* Jews aren't as sure as you think, Sabra. With all you Arabs wanting us dead, we worry we wandered too many years. We fear it's only you who belong. So *tell* me!

(She's lowered the gun, frightened.)

ABE: About Sabra.

SABRA: *(Choked)* You don't want to know.

ABE: That's right! But I have *no* choice.

(Frightened by his fierceness, and by approaching the story, she nearly whispers, fast—)

SABRA: It wasn't Israelis. You're right. They kept their hands clean. They only opened the gates.

ABE: *(Hoarse, holding off the experience as long as he can)* It was Christians, Sabra. It was Christians who went into Sabra.

(She looks at him, drawing into herself, and telling a simple story, with no emotion.)

SABRA: I'd gone to the edge of the camp for bread. The babies were crying, hungry again. Angry Timur, just three, and Somaya, who'd sucked Mama dry. I saw Israeli tanks lined up by the fence. The firing didn't scare me much. There was always shooting. I scuttled from shadow to shadow, past sundown now, curfew already, but I got through. I was skinny as a shadow.

On our alley, soldiers were banging at Aruri's, shouting "open up," and that frightened me. I could hear muffled screams down the alley. A man ran past. A shot flashed beside me. He fell, but I wasn't surprised, only wanting to get home fast. Darting, I came to our door, put my hand in the light flowing out. I was glad it cracked open, but about to scold Mama for not barring it tight, when I heard her moan—a deep terrible sound—then I saw. I saw past the soldier's legs to where little Timur was spread on the floor, opened, like a messy fountain, bubbling bright red.

ABE: No, Sabra, no...

SABRA: My mouth opened, but nothing came out. A hatchet hung from the soldier's fist. Mama was pressed to the wall clutching Somaya; I heard her—"I swear, this one's a girl."

(As SABRA quietly goes on speaking, and Abe stares dully ahead, his hands slowly rise, gradually sliding up, pressing both sides of his face.)

SABRA: But he tore the baby from Mama, and grunting, hurled her against the wall. "Girls become mothers. Mothers breed sons." Then he brought down his iron-spiked boot, hard on Somaya's face. I shrieked "Mama!" and jumped for his boot in the air, but he whacked me off with his hatchet, and thumped again with his spike, and again, and again, mashing her tiny face. Then he must have been tired, for he twisted back, and swung his hatchet only once more, slicing my Mama's belly straight through. She bent her head forward without a sound. I crawled to her lap. It was warm a long time.

(Finished, SABRA sits silent. Released from the story, ABE finally lets his head drop forward, his hands slide away. Silent, ABE lifts his head, looks at SABRA, wanting to help her, tries to speak—)

ABE: *(Hoarse)* Um Sa'ad...

SABRA: Um Sa'ad found me in Mama's lap. I let her wash me. But I didn't speak...for seven years.

ABE: *(Long pause. Then, quietly, the last word)* But life...didn't end.

(SABRA looks at him, her face clears, as though released. Her hand may reach slightly toward him, as though she would touch his face.)

SABRA: Sa'ad and Hamid were good to me, while they stayed. But now, Um Sa'ad only rocks on her stoop and talks about olives. She doesn't remember this dead life. She only dreams of home.

ABE: Sabra...Stay with me.

SABRA: *(Pause. Still looking at him)* A lost home is a kind of disease, you know. It drains off your soul.

ABE: I know.

SABRA: Some people leave their homes. Or deny them. But they're never lost.

ABE: No.

SABRA: *(Beginning to feel life)* So I promised her I'd go, I'd find it. And if I get to Jerusalem, the others can come.

ABE: You'll die, Sabra. How far can you get?

SABRA: *(Clear, happy)* I can't tell. The land will know me. When I touch it... I'll be alive. And the joy...! *(She breaks off, imagining the moment.)*

ABE: You're going to kill people.

SABRA: I won't if they let me pass. I'll warn them.

ABE: If you warn them, they'll shoot you. You'll explode alone.

SABRA: But they'll know it's my home. Why else would I die just to get there?

(He stares at her, then bursts out.)

ABE: You're insane!

SABRA: Am I? *Think.* If you were me? What would you do.

(He looks at her, without an answer. Pause. Then SABRA *picks up* ABE's *radio, and his rifle, and begins to move out.)*

ABE: If you take my rifle...

SABRA: If I leave it, you'll shoot me.

(He turns away sharply, and she's sorry for saying it.)

SABRA: You'd have to shoot me. Do you want the choice?

ABE: *(Pause)* I'll be naked out here.

(She glances around, disturbed.)

ABE: Your "brothers" will be happy to find me.

SABRA: *(Quickly)* I'll leave it a hundred yards out, against a tree. You can make it that far.

ABE: But the radio. You'll be safer if you wait till they call me.

SABRA: *(Considers the radio in her hand, nervous)* No, you'll tell them. You'll trick me.

ABE: If they call and don't reach me, they'll know something's wrong.

SABRA: They'll come just as fast either way.

ABE: But they'll bring more men.

SABRA: Shut up! You can't stop me!

ABE: That's right! *(He breaks)* Oh, Sabra, my little one, my love, wait. Just wait. I'll think of something. Please.

SABRA: Abraham...

ABE: *(Suddenly clear)* I'll take you to Jerusalem!

(She stares at him, astonished an instant, then shouts:)

SABRA: Don't say that!

(She's about to weep, he lurches toward her, pulling her to her knees, with him, on the quilt.)

ABE: Yes, yes, please, listen my love. *(He embraces her, ignoring the rifle and radio she holds.)*

ABE: Don't...don't cry, it's over now. That's what we'll do. I'll take you there. We'll go together.

SABRA: *(Clear, quiet)* You can't.

ABE: Why not?

SABRA: You know you can't.

ABE: What can't I do? If I love you, I can do anything.

SABRA: *(Staring at him, calm, backing away)* You're speaking like a child.

ABE: Maybe. Maybe it needs a child. Then that's what I'll be.

SABRA: Don't try to...

ABE: Let me take you. We'll find the tree together, the old wall, the eggplants.

SABRA: *(Gutteral, pained)* Abraham...

ABE: That's how it should be. I know the way.

SABRA: Please...

ABE: The air is so light there. It chimes. On the hillside, we could sing, we could make a child....

SABRA: You're talking magic. Don't! It's not fair!

ABE: Magic does happen. Do you believe I love you?

SABRA: *(Looks at him, deep, careful—)* In this moment...yes.

ABE: Then, in this moment, I can do whatever it takes.

SABRA: What can you do?

ABE: I don't know. We have to think, we have to plan.

(He holds her, and she him.)

ABE: Oh my love. *(Then takes her by the shoulders)* The first thing is.... We have to.... *(Embarrassed laugh)* ...unhook you. I can't hold onto a fully armed bomb.

SABRA: *(Backing away, a bit wary)* Don't...don't worry. The connection isn't live. I didn't hook it yet.

ABE: Let me see at least, Sabra.

(Still staying away from him, she lifts her shirt, revealing the belt, the packs in place, and the ignition pack in the center of her belly. He inhales sharply, nearly unnerved.)

ABE: Let's take it off, please.

SABRA: Not...not yet. I don't think we....

ABE: You don't believe me.

SABRA: I don't know if you can do what you say.

ABE: But you want me to.

SABRA: It's a dream. I don't think...

ABE: You're awake, Sabra. We both are.

SABRA: How? How could we...go there?

ABE: First, it has to seem natural. We'll say you're Lebanese, and I met you before I...

SABRA: No! They can't see me! I won't. They'll lock me up.

ABE: Why? Did you do something else?

SABRA: No, Abraham. I don't have to "do something" to get locked up. Hamid didn't "do something."

ABE: But we can tell them....

SABRA: No! It's impossible. They'll never let me in.

(The radio crackles, in her hand. They stare at each other.)

RADIO: Control to Abe. Control to Abe.

(She twists, about to run, but he grabs her.)

ABE: I'm going to marry you, Sabra.

(Stopped, she looks at him, hands him the radio, and backs off. While she watches him, and he her, she hooks up the wires on her belt. Controlling his alarm, ABE speaks into the radio.)

ABE: Abe here. You're up early. Is...is Benny...

RADIO: Benny hung on. He may make it.

ABE: *(Involuntary shout)* Oh God. God, God!

RADIO: You all right?

(SABRA is just now hooking up the wires.)

ABE: Great shape. About to hop in there.

RADIO: Stay where you are. We're on the way.

ABE: Roger. *(He lowers the radio, and spreads his arms.)* You can kill me now. They'll never know what happened.

(She holds, looking at him, then suddenly runs to him, embraces him.)

ABE: Careful. Careful with you. I'm not going to let you go, not going to let anyone hurt you. Do you understand me?

SABRA: Yes.

ABE: If you won't face them, then you'll have to hide. We'll have to meet later.

SABRA: Not here. You can't come here alone. And even if you could, then what? There's no way to "take" me there.

ABE: Can you get to Tyre?

SABRA: I got here. I guess...I can get anywhere.

ABE: I don't like it. There's too much chance to lose you.

SABRA: Yes.

ABE: I'll get you papers. A passport.

SABRA: *(Gasps, overjoyed)* A passport! A real passpo...

ABE: You know it couldn't be...

(He hesitates, she finishes the thought.)

SABRA: ...Palestinian. *(Quietly)* No. There's no such thing.

ABE: It would have to say...

SABRA: *(Interrupting)* It's no good, Abraham. You'd ruin your life.

ABE: *My* life?

SABRA: You'd be a traitor. Someone would know. And any Israeli who knows would do anything to stop you, anything. Terrible things would happen, against your will. And they'd never let me live.

ABE: *(Amused at her)* Israelis aren't as bad as you believe.

SABRA: It can't work. As soon as I do something, anything you don't like, you'll turn on me. You'd never trust me.

ABE: *(Shouts)* Stop insulting me!

SABRA: There's no time, Abraham. They're getting close. Just let me hide. I've come this far.

ABE: *(Frustrated, it bursts out)* I can't leave you loose here!

SABRA: Yes, that's it. I might betray you. Well, maybe you'll have to shoot me.

SABRA: *(Offers him his rifle, and her revolver)* If I give you this? If I hide? Will you still be afraid I'll hurt someone?

ABE: *(Taking the rifle, roughly)* Besides you, you mean?

SABRA: So it's your duty to shoot me. *(Pause, waiting for him to do it)* You better not tell them anything about us. They'll think you went mad.

ABE: Stop it! *(He lunges for her, grabs her.)*

SABRA: Be careful, I'm live!

ABE: Stop wasting the time! I'm not letting you go. I'm going to take you to Jerusalem, even if we have to cross the border under machine guns! So stop this. You've got to trust me!

SABRA: *(Anguished)* There is no way, Abraham.

ABE: Listen. Listen quickly. I know you've known only nightmares. But I'm strong. My only nightmare is fighting your fear. I have my home. My strength is enough for us both. You have to believe in me, now, believe we have hope.

(She's quiet. He kisses her.)

ABE: I'm going to find out where they are. *(Calls on the radio, holding her, looking at her)* Abe to Control.

RADIO: Control to Abe. Afraid we'll sneak up on you?

ABE: Where are you?

RADIO: Just passing Beaufort Castle. You'll hear us any minute. All clear?

ABE: Everything's quiet. Thanks. *(Clicks off radio, holds her quietly, speaks clearly)* Get me a sealed message. Bring it to I D F Central in Tyre, addressed to...

(She's watching him hopefully. Getting an idea, grins at her)

ABE: My boot! Hand me the bloody boot.

SABRA: What?

ABE: My boot...for this useless foot.

(She darts for the ruined boot, and holds it out to him, not understanding.)

ABE: Here's who you want to find. *(Draws out his dog tag)* But I'm keeping half of it.

(He breaks it in two, and hands her the half on the string.)

ABE: Half stays with the body, half goes...elsewhere.

SABRA: *(Holds him tight)* Oh, Abraham.

ABE: In the message, just tell me where you'll be next Saturday, all day. I'll get leave and a ride there. Anywhere you say. Do you believe me?

SABRA: *(Calm)* Yes.

ABE: Unhook this now.

(She looks at him uncertainly.)

ABE: Please. I won't ask you to take it off. Only...to take care of my love.

(She carefully disarms the ignition pack.)

ABE: Now answer me something.

SABRA: *(Smiles)* What can I answer you?

ABE: If you hadn't planned to die today...would you have made love to me last night?

SABRA: *(Sober)* Of course not!

(He laughs, holding her, rocking her.)

ABE: I don't even know how to feel about that. Sabra...Sabra...

SABRA: How will you take me to Jerusalem, Abraham?

ABE: As my wife. Don't you see? You can be anyone.

SABRA: Anyone?

ABE: Of course.

SABRA: Even an Israeli's wife.

ABE: Even that.

SABRA: But not...Palestinian.

ABE: Sabra, Sabra...no one can make you anyone but who you are.

SABRA: But if I pretend, I can be happy. *(Beat)* What about Um Sa'ad. *(Beat. Then, calmly, knowing—)* It's no good, is it. If I don't touch the land on my own, I haven't done anything. I've abandoned them all.

ABE: No you haven't. Not if you're happy.

SABRA: That's your love speaking.

ABE: Yes!

SABRA: *(Smiling, kisses him)* You're so strong. My invincible enemy. And I can rest, you'll always protect me...because you love me.

ABE: Yes.

SABRA: *(Gently pulling away from him)* Then you'll understand.

(Noise, of several people moving. She hears, and turns to go.)

ABE: *(A reflex, not understanding)* Don't go...

SABRA: I have to, Abraham. Please forgive me.

ABE: What? You have to stay here.

SABRA: Um Sa'ad needs her joy back. Listen my love. If I live and get there, she'll know she exists.

ABE: Please... It's too late to go.

SABRA: I'll be all right. I'l go quickly; I'll make it, don't worry.

ABE: You can't.

SABRA: I won't forget you, Abraham. I married you here.

(She runs to the hill. Muffled calls, off—)

DOG-STAR: *(Off)* Abe, are you there? Advise...Abe?! What's going on?

(SABRA climbs the hill, fast, will disappear running.)

ABE: Come back!

DOG-STAR: *(Alarmed cry, off)* Abe, where are you? Halt!

ABE: Don't shoot, don't shoot!!

(Shots off. Then a dull explosion, from the direction SABRA ran)

(ABE drops to his knees, arms spread. His face is contorted in a scream we don't hear.)

(As the lights fade, until only the glow of the explosion remains, we hear GRAMMA speaking in Hebrew, then overlaid in English, then in Arabic....)

GRAMMA: ...Surely goodness and mercy shall follow me all the days of my life, and I will dwell in the house of the Lord for ever.

(Blackout)

END OF PLAY

TRUTH TAKES A HOLIDAY

TRUTH TAKES A HOLIDAY, under the title TRUTH OR DARE, had a concert reading at LaMama La Galeria on 25 March 2000. The cast and creative contributors were:

JACK .... Bill Bartlett
NORA .... Cathy Schaeffer
RUSS .... Peter McCabe
KAT .... Florencia Lozano
Stage directions .... Jim Seaman
Director .... George Ferencz

CHARACTERS & SETTING

Russ *and* Kat *are advisors, respectively, to President* Jack *and first lady* Nora.

Jack. *Natural king. Has gifts of mind, ambition, vision, tripped by unruly child's heart. Husband to* Nora. *40s.*

Nora. *Brilliant. Appealing warmth and spirit. Her fires dangerously banked in support of leader she believes in. Wife to* Jack. *40s.*

Russ. *The rock. His wry wisdom seasons his passion; he bears all, understands all, could never be front man. Friend to* Jack *and* Nora. *40s.*

Kat. *Talented political analyst promoted to job of her dreams. Sensual, witty, empathetic, with plenty to learn. 30s.*

Three open playing areas—the First Lady's, the President's, an advisor's area between.

A desk or writing table and chair in each area. Phones in each, a lounge for Nora, *a roll-on T V. Light through large windows.*

The action flows easily from one area to another.

ACT ONE

(At the top, we see JACK *in the entrance to* NORA's *room.)*

JACK: It's not true.

*(*NORA *looks at him.)*

JACK: Nora. *(Pause)* Please...

(She turns toward a window.)

JACK: God damn it, you've got to believe me.

*(*NORA *glances at him, and away.)*

NORA: *(Quietly)* Please go.

JACK: Nora...

*(*NORA *walks swiftly to her desk, presses; we hear intercom—)*

VOICE-OVER: Yes?

NORA: The President is leaving. Put through my call.

*(*JACK *walks swiftly toward her, but seeing her face as she looks up at him, he stops, facing her. The phone rings.* NORA *doesn't move to answer.* JACK *and* NORA *face each other. Phone rings again.* JACK *turns and leaves.* NORA *still doesn't move. The phone rings again.)*

VOICE-OVER: I have your son on the line. Do you...?

*(*NORA *picks up the phone, near tears, but controlling herself.)*

NORA: Hi honey. How'd the calculus go? ... Don't worry—it's the first premise that's impossible. Once that clicks for you, it gets easier. ... No, I'm fine. Just got a moment free, and... Honey, there's going to be some more...character attacks in the news, and...Jody, listen—we're fine. ...Yes, but you can't help what people say. So we'll have to. ... Good idea. *(A little laugh)* Yeah, news blackout. Think I'll try it. Bye, now. ... I'll tell him. Love you too.

*(*NORA *puts down the phone with a sob, and collapses, weeping.)*

(In advisor's area, RUSS *is finishing a phone call,* KAT *leaned over him.)*

RUSS: All right, I'll tell him.

*(*RUSS *hangs up the phone, getting up from his desk.)*

KAT: What's going on?

RUSS: I don't have time, Kat.

KAT: Where are these accusations coming from?

RUSS: *(Gathering papers)* We don't know yet. It's all "a source close to so and so."

KAT: Well, what are you going to...? Straighten your tie, Russ.

(JACK *is in the entrance.*)

JACK: Well?

RUSS: David says "Say nothing."

JACK: He's wrong. We've got to move fast.

RUSS: Mr President. We can't say a word.

JACK: I've got to deny this. Nip it in the bud. How will it look if we wait? It's ridiculous! Stop it now. *(Snaps his fingers)* Like that.

RUSS: *(Patiently)* If we deny it, we'll have to explain their so-called evidence, and then they'll not only see what we have, we won't have time to gather anything else.

KAT: Uuuuh.

RUSS: Our case is stronger if we wait.

JACK: I can't take it!

RUSS: You've got to. We don't know how big this is.

JACK: What do you mean—"how big"?

(KAT *is gathering her calendar, and, as they go on, will quickly leave.*)

RUSS: How many people are involved, how they've put this together....

JACK: With crepe paper and chicken wire! It's gone with the first strong wind!

RUSS: So we give them enough news time, and they'll hang themselves.

JACK: Meantime who's running the country?

RUSS: You are. And we've got to let David do *his* job! Understood?

(JACK *doesn't answer. He's staring ahead, thinking.*)

RUSS: How's Nora? *(Pause)* Sir?

JACK: What do you think?

RUSS: Talk to her. If she buckles, nobody's going to blame the media. They'll say it's because it's true.

JACK: I've tried. I... *(His voice chokes.)*

RUSS: Jack. She loves you.

JACK: Is that a reason to trust me?

(KAT *is bent over* NORA, *applying tea bags to her eyes.*)

KAT: Frozen bags. Works every time. Breathe deep.

(NORA *leaned back, takes a deep breath.*)

KAT: So they're at it again.

NORA: Yeah.

KAT: Playing your song?

NORA: Couldn't catch us in a crime...

KAT: *(Checking* NORA's *eyes)* 'At a girl.

NORA: So they're back to the old "divide and conquer."

KAT: Not even a smudge. Let's hit your itinerary.

(KAT *opens her calendar.* NORA *is resting.*)

NORA: How am I going to survive, Kat? Othello didn't. *(Beat)* And he was a big strong warrior.

KAT: *(Reading the calendar)* With only Iago to set him up. Not every Republican right of center.

NORA: And Desdemona was innocent!

KAT: She still died.

NORA: *(Groaning)* Tell me about it.

KAT: O K—only three major appearances today.

NORA: Oh, lord—media.

KAT: Let's see where there'll be press....

NORA: Thank God it's Friday.

KAT: This won't be hard. Business women's caucus, dedication of the servicewomen's museum, visit to Children's Hospital. You might get some intrusive questions at the caucus, but otherwise they're soft situations. Just be charming and calm. The usual. Like... "I'm not familiar with these charges, but after what they've already tried, nothing would surprise me."

NORA: Do they think he's an imbecile?! Why do we have to listen to this. For god's sake, we're working every second. When would he have the time?

KAT: Well, Iago didn't need logic. Just a drop of doubt—toss a dirty innuendo at an innocent exchange, and Bingo! Murder, suicide, fire, and flood.

(RUSS *enters.*)

RUSS: Morning, Nora. Could you excuse us a minute, Kat?

KAT: *(Checks her watch)* We're already behind.

RUSS: A second. I promise.

(KAT *gives him a "don't rock a leaky boat" gesture, and exits.*)

NORA: *(Looks at* RUSS. *Quietly—)* Yes?

RUSS: I just want to...brief you.

NORA: "Brief me"? On what to say?

RUSS: On what they know—*think* they know.

NORA: I can't listen to this. And I don't have time.

RUSS: Nora, they'll question you.

NORA: What about? Somebody's claiming he had an affair? What else is new?

RUSS: The special prosecuter is moving on it.

NORA: What?!

RUSS: Because there's a tape.

NORA: *(Freezes)* Tape?

RUSS: Apparently.

NORA: Of Jack?

RUSS: No. Of the girl, talking to a friend.

NORA: Then it's nothing!

RUSS: Nora...

NORA: I've had it with this!

RUSS: It won't help to get angry.

NORA: Do you know how they come at him? How they push and drool? What does the press expect? Of course, one of them's gone crazy. I'll bet there's a dozen out there who'd tell you they've worn my pajamas!

RUSS: Be that as it may...

NORA: Who is she?

RUSS: *(Beat)* Laurinda Wells.

NORA: Who?

RUSS: There's a picture here.... *(Picking up newspaper)*

NORA: *(Looking at it)* I don't think I...

RUSS: It's blurred.

NORA: *(Recognizing the girl)* I... Yes. I remember her....

(NORA's *getting images of Laurinda, and nausea is welling up.*)

RUSS: She was a college...

NORA: *(Shallow breaths)* Yes...here a lot, very...determined.

RUSS: Nora, are you O K?

NORA: I'm all right. I...

(Nausea overcomes NORA, until she releases it in violent vomiting, as she collapses forward. RUSS runs to support her.)

(In advisor's space, JACK is coordinating itineraries with KAT.)

JACK: I've got this banquet at noon, but I want lunch with Nora.

KAT: She's got the Children's Hospital fund drive. And we're already delayed.

JACK: All right, later then.

KAT: Let me see... *(Checking NORA's schedule)*

JACK: How's she doing, Kat?

KAT: Great. Russ is in, briefing her on the...problem.

JACK: Jesus.

KAT: How about four-thirty? Should be at least twenty minutes there.

JACK: Have to do. Stay with her?

KAT: What else? *(Beat)* Sir?

JACK: This goddamn junior-grade bitch!

KAT: Don't say it. You'll be quoted.

JACK: Right. Thanks.

(JACK exits. KAT checks her watch, moving in to join NORA.)

KAT: Briefing done? Are we "go" here?

RUSS: *(Sheepish)* I could, uh, use your help.

(NORA lying back, pale, still)

KAT: Oh, no...

NORA: *(Quietly)* Cool rag, please?

KAT: Coming up. *(Moves quickly to dip a napkin in ice water)* What happened?

RUSS: Well, she just...

(Silence, till KAT reaches NORA with the napkin, and sees her face.)

KAT: Oh my god.

NORA: Nothing suicide won't cure.

KAT: Baby.

NORA: Can't always suppress your gut feeling, you know? Sometimes it just...makes the statement for you.

KAT: Nobody's going anywhere till you feel better.

NORA: Funny. When you've already been to a bad place, you think you'd develop some armor.

KAT: If you're an armadillo. *(Blaming him)* That's probably enough, Russell.

(RUSS *edges out, will hover outside.*)

KAT: *(Into her phone)* Judy? Delay.

NORA: I can't take this, Kat, I can't take it again....

KAT: I know.

NORA: I don't know how to stop this hurt. And I just...

KAT: *(Pause)* What happened?

NORA: *(Quiet)* When I saw her picture it cut into me...that it could be true—like a blade straight to the lung. You know, it takes your breath, and you actually think you're dying.

(NORA's *breathing with difficulty, bewildered. She looks at* KAT, *who squeezes her hand.*)

NORA: You know what that's like?

KAT: *(Watching her, frightened)* No.

NORA: Must be partly shock...because something your system can't accept is happening. Then it's like you're unhooked, like a body snatching. Because the person you trust with your life has become someone who's killing you.

KAT: *(Reaching for her)* Baby, it's not true.

NORA: *(Quickly)* And more than anything, you want to change him back, so things can be like they were. But your mind tells you—and this is what's unbearable—it tells you *he never was* the person you thought he was. Reality's who he is now. I have to accept it.

KAT: Nora...

NORA: *(Simply)* Betrayal.

KAT: But it's not...

NORA: And love is gone. Instantly. As if he'd been killed.

KAT: No.

NORA: Yes, you know love's gone, but it won't let go. It keeps clinging, begging you to let it live. *(Beat)* Then comes humiliation. Because he has, by his betrayal, insulted and harmed you. You are ridiculous. You need to hate him. But you love him. And he's making you rip love out of your soul.

That's the greatest violation. That's the shock. Everything in you wants to survive and not feel pain. You want desperately to love him, but you mustn't. He made you vulnerable, then destroyed you. *(Beat)* So your sanity wavers. A moment ago you were safe and cared for. Now you're battered, at total risk, and if you show your face, they see a fool.

(Speechless, KAT looks to RUSS, in the door; he signals. NORA closes her eyes. KAT goes to RUSS; they speak low—)

RUSS: She's scheduled to visit her mom?

KAT: Yes, for the weekend. Has she changed her mind?

RUSS: No. That's just it.

NORA: *(From her couch)* Change my flight time, Kat. In case it was released.

RUSS: That won't look good.

NORA: But it feels good. It's the only thought that'll get me through the day.

RUSS: Not a good idea.

KAT: If she does anything but what she planned, you'll give them fuel. They'll broadcast the change as emergency tactics.

RUSS: Nobody's going to remember this visit was "planned". They're going to say she's running home to Mama.

(KAT pauses, looking at RUSS. NORA is sitting up, shaky, determined.)

NORA: I've got to get out of here.

RUSS: Please Nora, in the interest of security.

NORA: No.

KAT: He's right, Nora. You've got to stay.

NORA: No!

(Abrupt change. Voice-overs as actors move. Scrim may display silhouettes of a hectic press conference, voices overlap.)

VOICE-OVER: The first lady has a full schedule today.

VOICE-OVER: When can we see her?

VOICE-OVER: I'm sorry she won't have time.

VOICE-OVER: What does she say about...?

VOICE-OVER: Is she going to encourage women to run in the next...?

VOICE-OVER: What does she say about the allegations of sexual misconduct on the part of the President?

VOICE-OVER: She's heard nothing about such a matter.

VOICE-OVER: When will Nora speak to us?!

(Angry KAT confronting RUSS, who's slowly going through papers.)

KAT: How could you *do* it!

RUSS: Calm down.

KAT: Do you know what even a *hint* that her man's unfaithful does to a woman?

RUSS: Don't condescend to me. I've been there before with Nora.

KAT: Then how could you make such an idiot move? At the beginning of a day!

RUSS: You underestimate her.

KAT: I don't underestimate a total upchuck!

RUSS: Stick your head under the tap, Kat. You're needed on square one.

KAT: Jesus.

(KAT flops down, puts her head between her legs. RUSS, calmly reflective—)

RUSS: It's the fast track, Kat. Business as usual. Front page every day.

KAT: I belong on a backroom keyboard, not planetary TV.

RUSS: You never thought, just 'cause you had a feel for the inside, were great at interviews...?

KAT: And organization, and deadlines...

RUSS: Once a journalist, always...

KAT: What does *that* mean?

RUSS: In my experience, your species never quite makes the leap, always keeps one toe on the observation platform.

KAT: God, if I leapt any farther, I'd hit bottom ahead of her. *(Gets up, pacing as though caged)* A person could suffocate. Why isn't there any air in this place?!

RUSS: For who?

KAT: It's surreal, Russ. *(Drops back, breathing deep, trying to calm)* Look at us—we've got Nora and Jack—national figures in distress—in our care. But if I start to blend, and live for her, it's....

RUSS: Just be glad there's no tenure.

KAT: But how will I ever come down? *(Beat)* When it's all over, will it self-erase, like a visit with aliens?

RUSS: Submit the idea, will you?

KAT: Why are you so goddamned cool?

RUSS: *(Stacking his papers)* Practice. You live longer.

KAT: Then what? A lifetime supply of Snickers? Don't tell me you do this for your wife and kids.

RUSS: No, they always pay. But the family's my oxygen tap in this stratosphere—where there's no air and no way of actually living, no everyday joys.

KAT: Gee, Russ, and you're such an everyday guy.

RUSS: *(Finishing off work)* Right. Up from the neighborhood, like his everyday socks.

KAT: Come on. Jack couldn't do without you.

RUSS: *(Packing up)* Course he could. *(Beat)* I've always suspected Jack's some kind of advanced organism, who spawns projections of himself to mind the store, so he can focus on the moment's priority.

KAT: Wooo.

RUSS: It's a future system for organizing power. I mean, given the pyramid is still our basic mode, he incorporates network in an inspired way, makes a pyramid shaped network. He couldn't bring it off without enormous confidence, and trust. *(Beat. Sees KAT staring)* You getting this down?

KAT: *(Smiling)* How bizarre—if his whole pyramid wobbles on the pin of a stray erection.

RUSS: *(Angry, gets up swiftly)* Take notes. Your memoirs'll sail you through retirement.

KAT: If they're ever declassified.

RUSS: *(On his way out)* Why bother, when you can leak it.

KAT: *(Stands, angry—)* Russell!

(KAT turns quickly to go after RUSS, but faces JACK.)

(Same: JACK, *rapidly approaching* KAT*)*

JACK: Nora isn't back? You said she'd have twenty minutes.

KAT: I'm sorry, Sir. We lost time getting off. So everything's running late.

JACK: I've got to talk to her. If we aren't careful this thing is going to get out of hand, and I need her to...

KAT: You've got to pull back. Trust me, Mr President, she...went to pieces.

JACK: No.

KAT: Bigtime. When Russ showed her Laurinda's picture.

JACK: *(Collapses into a chair)* Uuuuh. *(Pause)* She doesn't believe it?

KAT: I don't know. It's like she's on every side—afraid to believe it, afraid to not believe it. And her gut can't help expect the worst.

JACK: *(Groan)* Yeah, I know. *(Silence. Then, relaxed —)* Funny. I'm tearing along, nose to grindstone, pumping on all cylinders, thinking it's very very good...and all of a sudden—a wet patch. From out of nowhere. Why? Was it lying in wait? If I'd seen it, could I have swerved? Was I wrong to think I could fly?

KAT: *(Pause)* Do you remember this...Laurinda?

JACK: Of course I do! She stuck herself in my face on an hourly basis. I finally had to get her a nice job *off* the premises.

KAT: Did Nora know that?

JACK: Why? Would she have liked it in her face, too?!

KAT: Sir.

JACK: *(Sighs)* All right, all right, I'll back off. A little. Be nice, Kat, be sweet to me. I need a rest. A little breather. Come on. You know how to make me laugh.

KAT: *(Flattered, she laughs.)* Jack...

JACK: See? Laughing's healthy. Right? And innocent. Right? Come on, now...

KAT: *(Trying a joke about him)* Did you hear the one about the President who was late to lunch?

JACK: *(Smiles a second, anticipating, then explodes)* God! I can't even laugh. Too many punch lines pop up to whack me! I'm a gaping bulls-eye! This big fat donkey everyone's trying to pin the tail on. And I'm terminally *sick* of it!

KAT: I'm sorry, sir.

JACK: *(Furious)* Just tell Nora I've got to see her right away.

(JACK *exits swiftly, upstage.* KAT *collapses back, fists on her temples.)*

(VOICE-OVERS *and scrim silhouettes)*

VOICE-OVER: Mr President?

VOICE-OVER: Mr President, did you have a relationship with Laurinda Wells?

VOICE-OVER: Mr President!

VOICE-OVER: Mr President. How will you answer the special prosecutor's allegations?

VOICE-OVER: Mr President, what are the normal duties of White House interns?

VOICE-OVER: Mr President?

(RUSS, *upset and exhausted, with bad news he'll try to keep to himself, enters advisors' space, joining* KAT, *who's at work with schedules.*)

RUSS: Still no Nora? *(Flops down)* I don't believe this. I just don't believe it!

KAT: That it could happen? Or that it did.

RUSS: *(Too dazed to hear straight; beat—)* You still here? Thought you had a life.

KAT: I haven't noticed. You?

RUSS: Forget it. Mary says I'm not even home when I'm home, so what's the difference?

KAT: Well...if you were going to quit, I'd suggest "yesterday" as the perfect moment.

RUSS: Now you tell me.

KAT: *(Pause)* Tell me something. How'd Jack respond when he first heard?

RUSS: About what?

KAT: The "Laurinda" matter.

RUSS: *(Thinks, then—)* Blank. Then he said "who?"

KAT: "Who" like he didn't remember? Or "who" like denial?

RUSS: Like he didn't remember. When I said there was a tape, he seemed puzzled. I think he said "Of what?"

KAT: He didn't look guilty?

RUSS: Come on. He doesn't know how.

KAT: Well, worried?

RUSS: Just tired.

KAT: *(Sighs)* What's going to happen, Russ?

RUSS: Another day, another crap shoot. You know that.

KAT: I know another weekend's shot. What's Mary going to say?

RUSS: Who's Mary?

KAT: Hmmh.

RUSS: I phoned. Asked her to fax me her picture.

KAT: *(Beat)* What if it's true, Russ?

RUSS: What?

KAT: What Laurinda says on the tape.

RUSS: Good god, Kat, make sense!

(KAT *doesn't answer.*)

RUSS: Do you think he's out of his mind?!

KAT: No. *(Beat)* I think he's male. I think he's arrogant. And reckless. And sexually driven.

RUSS: You think he's out of his mind.

KAT: I think he can't keep it in his pants!

RUSS: *(Stares at her)* Why are women so quick to believe the worst?

KAT: *(Shrugs)* Experience.

RUSS: Be serious a minute!

KAT: I'm scared to be, Russ!

RUSS: Just consider the source.

KAT: All right. An over-stuffed, salivating groupie...

RUSS: ...who fantasizes.

KAT: Yeah. That's where the mind goes. Instantly. At least a woman's does.

RUSS: Careful, you'll lose your P C rating.

KAT: I'm being honest. Fantasizing, I can imagine. And being so insecure she blubbers to friends about it, to make herself interesting. Of course, if *you* say that you're sexist.

RUSS: But I am. Card-carrying.

KAT: No, really. Because men always think women are fantasizing. Especially about them.

RUSS: When you aren't?

KAT: Of course we aren't. Fantasies are reserved for the big guns we can't handle.

RUSS: Can I enter that statement in evidence, Kathleen?

KAT: Whatever you want. But a fantasy can be *intense*—and scary.

RUSS: This is experience talking?

KAT: Not lately. But when eroticism grabbed me, at about twelve, I developed a fantasy life that overlapped reality so far that when something real did occur with a boy, I couldn't tell if it actually happened. That's how intense my mind-life was.

RUSS: "Mind-life."

KAT: Ever had one?

RUSS: Sure. But I think boys at that age are more...object focused, you know?

KAT: *This* boy was not on the page. But he did make a few right moves.

RUSS: But our Laurinda is past adolescence.

KAT: Barely. And she's very likely frustrated. And certainly spoiled.

RUSS: And psychologically...I hate to say...challenged?

KAT: Lord help us. Tell me he couldn't!

RUSS: I'd love to! *(Silence)* She could do us in, Kat. The whole mountain—could come tumbling down.

KAT: I know.

RUSS: She's practically a minor!

KAT: *(Looks at RUSS, pause—)* You're over-dramatizing.

RUSS: I don't think it's possible, Kat. If there's even a hint this is true...

KAT: There'll be a deluge?

RUSS: Like Noah never dreamed of.

(NORA interrupts them, standing in an entrance. She's still shaken, but in command, calm.)

NORA: Kat...

KAT: *(On her feet)* You're back! And looking good. Meetings went O K?

NORA: Still on my feet. *(Beat)* Kat. Starting now, I want to hear everything.

KAT: *(Wary)* Everything?

NORA: Every news item, or piece of information, related to the Wells matter.

KAT: Forgive me, but...that's an all-time terrible idea. Sure way to lose your mind. No.

NORA: Kat—Every. Single. Report.

KAT: Why?! You know it's what they want—to get you strung out.

NORA: What "they" want doesn't matter.

KAT: You're playing straight into their hands.

NORA: Who'll know I'm playing?

KAT: It's a painful drug, Nora.

RUSS: She's right, Nora.

KAT: And it'll get worse. Sleaze sells!

NORA: If I don't know what they're saying, and, in fact, everything there is to know, I won't know what I'm up against. Will I?

(NORA holds a beat, looking at KAT and RUSS, neither of whom know how to answer, then turns to exit.)

KAT: *(Recovering her voice)* Uhh, Nora?

NORA: Yes.

KAT: When Jack gets back, can I send him in?

NORA: *(Stopped, she looks blank an instant.)* I think....

(KAT and Russ are strained forward, hoping she'll agree.)

NORA: ...I better... Please tell him I... Tell him no. *(She quietly leaves.)*

KAT: *(Collapsing back)* Oooh no.

RUSS: Sorry.

(Silence)

KAT: Why do we do this?

RUSS: Fame. Riches. Full medical benefits.

KAT: Thanks. *(Pause)* Is Jack going to make a statement?

RUSS: No.

KAT: He's got to! It's flying out of hand. If he doesn't squelch it right now...

RUSS: David says "Don't discuss Laurinda." Absolutely. There's nothing so powerful as keeping a closed hand. Especially when they're bluffing.

KAT: That's fine for court. What about public opinion? A man who won't say he's innocent is guilty! Especially where sex is involved. Even if he only thought about it.

RUSS: Isn't that only with Catholics?

KAT: A man is *always* guilty.

RUSS: Don't be a bitch.

KAT: Well, maybe not every man. There's true blue Russell—stalwart lion by the gate.

RUSS: *Can* it!

KAT: Sorry. Terror makes me giddy.

(Stony silence)

RUSS: So she's condemning him without a trial?

KAT: She's shell-shocked. You saw her. It's an old wound.

RUSS: What will you tell her?

KAT: Whatever I hear.

RUSS: Christ!

KAT: Doesn't she deserve to know? Do you think she's stupid?

RUSS: So help me, Kat...

KAT: Well, you've known them longer than anybody. You ought to have an opinion.

RUSS: *(Trying to hold in, finally losing it)* I think...Pandora's bursting open. This is a nightmare we could die from, and I don't want to be in it one more second! *(Brings him to his feet)*

KAT: *(Startled by his passion)* Wow. So much for "stay cool, you'll live longer". Come on, Russ. We'll get in there—tone down the special effects. That's our job, isn't it?

RUSS: *(Hands on his head)* Long as we have one.

KAT: Just...cool it now. Sit back down here, and give me all of it. What are you sitting on? That Nora and I don't know.

RUSS: *(Looks hard at* KAT, *collapses with a sigh)* They've subpoenaed the White House records on Laurinda Wells.

KAT: *(Groans)* Oooh, goodie.

RUSS: We've found lots of visits. By her. Even after she left the job.

KAT: *(Curt)* So. *(Pause)* And what are you not telling me?

RUSS: What are you asking?

KAT: Could this...have happened without your knowing about it?

RUSS: No! *(Beat)* Could what.

KAT: Je-sus!

RUSS: No.

KAT: No. *(Nods. Pause)* Is that all?

RUSS: There are memos.

KAT: That's routine.

RUSS: If they aren't equivocal.

KAT: Are they?

RUSS: No.

KAT: How would you know? *(Pause)* Russ?

RUSS: And there are gifts.

KAT: *(Choked)* What...kind of gifts?

RUSS: Routine. Far as we've found.

KAT: I'm getting sick.

RUSS: Catching, isn't it.

(They look at each other.)

---

*(*JACK *enters. Cool, unperturbed)*

JACK: Good. Nora's back?

KAT: Uh, no, sir. She...doesn't want to be disturbed.

JACK: What?

KAT: I'm sorry.

(JACK, *hit by the blow, looks in* NORA's *direction, deciding whether to defy her wish.*)

RUSS: I think it's better, sir...for now.

JACK: *(Looks hard at* RUSS. *Pause)* I was hoping...

RUSS: Yeah.

JACK: Did she...say anything?

KAT: She wants to be apprised of every detail we get.

JACK: That's good.

RUSS: And every report.

JACK: You mean, commentary?

KAT: I tried to stop her.

JACK: She'll go out of her mind!

KAT: I argued.

RUSS: She did. We both argued.

(JACK *stares at them like a caged lion—unable to spring, then springs the only way he can, pacing—*)

KAT: Tell us what we can do; where are we?

JACK: Well. David has decided, because of the...media storm, that it's all right—even could be advantageous—for me to be interviewed on The Newshour.

RUSS: That's fantastic! Presidential spotlight.

KAT: Use your clout to grab focus—brilliant.

JACK: Yeah. *(He sits heavily, staring, unstrung, needing company. Pause)*

RUSS: Could be worse. Could be *my* turn at debate.

JACK: Yeah.

KAT: Debate?

RUSS: Yeah. I'd always have the best data....

JACK: Most persuasive arguments, most forthright, honest case...

RUSS: And I'd get up, get a red face, drop my notes....

JACK: Forget about it.

RUSS: Complete loss.

JACK: *(Pause)* I look all right?

KAT: Great. You're the man.

RUSS: Are you set?

JACK: Raring to go. Got a fraudulent ambush to dispense with, right? Ka-pow!

KAT: You tell 'em, Mr President.

RUSS: Dose of cold reason. That's perfect.

JACK: Nora likes this tie. Calls it my Abe Lincoln look.

KAT: Very presidential.

JACK: Honest Abe. *(Beat)* I need her, Kat. *(He's walking away.)*

KAT: Then go get her. I'll see she watches.

(JACK *walks upstage into a spotlight.*)

(KAT *puts her hand out to* RUSS *as they watch* JACK *go. They stand nervous, as though waiting in the wings.*)

KAT: Now remind me why do we do it?

RUSS: Dumb question. Better government.

KAT: Oh, yeah?

RUSS: How young are you? Remember a president with intelligence?

KAT: But will you give it your life?

RUSS: Don't ask.

KAT: What if you had to choose—Mary or him.

RUSS: Not even funny.

KAT: Yeah. I wanted excitement, but this is ridiculous.

RUSS: People want different things.

KAT: Specifically, maybe. But in general, we're the same bizarre mix of needs.

RUSS: Oh?

KAT: It's just that our drugs differ.

RUSS: So you tell me. Why are we doing it?

KAT: Don't know. Move us a fraction closer to civilization?

RUSS: *(Tight laugh)* Civilization.

KAT: Could be the last chance.

RUSS: *(Leaving)* For god's sake...

KAT: Well...when it's flying apart you've got to focus somewhere.
(She stands alone, watching.)

(Lights change. Applause. NORA *comes downstage to join* KAT, *switches on a television that faces upstage, and they watch what may also be on scrim, upstage.)*

KAT: He's going to shut them up.

NORA: I hope so.

KAT: You kidding? When he puts on that earnest face. The serenity, with just a touch of the wounded...

NORA: It's not put on.

KAT: Whatever. It works. Watch.

*(*RUSS *comes down quickly to join them.)*

RUSS: Is he on?

KAT: Shhhh. *(To* NORA*)* You O K?

*(*NORA *takes Kat's hand. They all watch as the interview begins.)*

RUSS: Good. Good opening.

KAT: That's it. The budget...Iraq...

NORA: I like the tie.

RUSS: Take stage—the buck stops here. And we want it that way!

KAT: Shhh, here it comes.

(They're all riveted, listening. We may hear a voice-over, but it's unintelligible.)

RUSS: Good. He looks at ease, pleasant, truthful....

KAT: That little smile does it. Not quite condescending. Just kind. A hint sad.

*(*KAT *and* RUSS *relax back, but* NORA *is increasingly worried.)*

NORA: What's he talking—legalese? "There is no relationship." Is? Is?!

KAT: Nora, shhh...

NORA: What's wrong with "Has never been. Is not and never was. Not in this life or the next!"

KAT: I'm sure he means...

NORA: Who cares, when he keeps saying "is"? Is he trying to look guilty?

KAT: I think he's trying to look calm, and dignified. And he's doing it.

RUSS: He expects that when the President says something, it will be believed.

NORA: Why? The one thing they all agree on is that he lies.

*(*RUSS *stares at* NORA, *says nothing, unwilling to argue.)*

KAT: But they trust him, Nora.

NORA: They say they *don't!*

(*Everyone silenced. Then—*)

RUSS: They trust him to make things right.

(NORA *stares at* RUSS.)

KAT: (*Trying to defuse the tension*) Why don't we just...see how it plays.

(NORA *looks at them both, then turns without a word, and exits.*)

(RUSS *sighs, collapses.*)

RUSS: Where are we?

KAT: He did look good. Have to wait for the commentary.

RUSS: I mean with Nora.

(KAT *looks at him, not knowing the answer, finally says—*)

KAT: It's going to be a long night.

RUSS: Jack's got to get back to work on his speech. We've lost a whole day. And he's tied in knots....

KAT: And Nora?

RUSS: She did notes on his first draft. But they haven't really got down to it.

KAT: Think we can count on quiet now?

RUSS: Depends what other shoes there are.

KAT: Left to drop.

RUSS: And how many.

KAT: Were we wrong to make Nora stay here?

RUSS: He needs her.

KAT: But if she won't see him?

RUSS: (*Looks at* KAT. *Beat—*) Then, yes. We were wrong.

KAT: (*Pause*) You remember the girl?

RUSS: Laurinda? Ohh, yes.

KAT: And?

RUSS: She got in his radar. Cheery, bouncy, always with a question. You know how he eats that up—the inquisitive young, the mind that's eager to learn. Then, there was always some special favor she thought to do. Like she was trying out for teacher's pet.

(RUSS *is silent, with his thoughts.*)

KAT: And?

RUSS: And what?

KAT: What do you think?

RUSS: I don't. I just pray.

(Silence)

RUSS: What are they saying now?

KAT: *(Focused on the T V)* They're wondering why he said "is."

(JACK enters energetically. RUSS and KAT rise to shake his hand.)

JACK: How'd it play?

RUSS: Presidential. Right on.

KAT: Good work, Mr President.

JACK: P B S was grateful. Feels like things may calm down. More to the point, David was pleased. 'Spose I can get back to my speech now?

RUSS: Hear, hear!

JACK: *(Looking around)* Nora?

KAT: She watched with us.

JACK: And?

KAT: Your guess is as good as mine.

RUSS: She's great with commentary.

JACK: Sure is.

KAT: If she'll give it.

JACK: Kat?

KAT: I don't know, Sir.

JACK: *(Beat)* Well. Nothing like the present.

(JACK moves away, toward NORA's area. RUSS and KAT watch him, tense.)

KAT: Did you ever actually ask him?

RUSS: What?

KAT: You know what.

RUSS: Of course I did.

KAT: And?

RUSS: He said, "Are you kidding?"

(NORA *is sitting alone by a window, in the dark.* JACK *is in a door, then crosses toward her. She doesn't seem to notice him.*)

JACK: *(Quietly)* What are you doing?

NORA: Waiting.

JACK: For...

NORA: To know, I guess.

JACK: What?

NORA: *(Pause)* What to do.

(JACK *sits beside her. She doesn't look at him. Pause*)

JACK: How was Jody's calculus?

NORA: Doesn't make sense to him.

JACK: If it did, we should worry. *(Looks for her smile. It doesn't come.)* Did you...talk to him about this?

NORA: Not the specifics. But I warned him.

(JACK *nods, choked.* NORA's *throat is tight.*)

NORA: He said to tell you to lead with your right.

JACK: *(Tries to laugh)* Yeah. *(In a knot, he gets up, paces, then stops, looks at* NORA.) How will you know...what to do?

NORA: *(Looks at him, can't answer.)* Was David pleased with the interview?

JACK: *(Thrown by her change of subject)* Yes. He was.

NORA: Good.

JACK: *(Pause)* How about you? *(No answer)* What did you think?

NORA: You looked fine. You sounded guilty.

JACK: How?

(NORA *looks at* JACK.)

JACK: The "is"?

NORA: Why on earth...?

JACK: David said "only those words." Nothing else. So it's simple, unequivocal.

NORA: "*Is* no relationship" infers that there was, but is no longer.

JACK: I know! I know that now.

NORA: Unless that's what you meant.

JACK: Don't.

NORA: What?

JACK: Don't do this.

NORA: Sit here with my guts torn out?

JACK: It's what they want. To break us. It's so flagrant, I don't know how they dare! David didn't even want me to dignify it with an answer. He kept talking me down, saying "Be mild. Stay mild." I would have exploded on camera!

(He looks at NORA, *but she's unreadable.)*

JACK: Nora. Will you get in the same room with me?

NORA: Which one?

JACK: The one where we're together! I can't take this from you too!

NORA: Jack, I...

JACK: If we let this happen, we're falling into their hands. They've thrown everything they could, dug up every old rock, and found nothing...*nothing* to hit us with. So this is their last, most treacherous move. Because if they succeed, if they divide us, we have lost our strength, and we will fall.

NORA: *(Pause)* You're saying, stand firm, so *we* won't fall?

JACK: Nora, the napkins won't stay neatly folded in the drawer. This is not tidy. You can't lay down limits and think people won't come breathing, stinking, swarming all over them. You've got to have the nerve to wing it.

NORA: "Wing" it?

JACK: This is going to be about you, Nora. I'm just the victim here. They'll smear me as far as their lies can take them. And how am I ever going to prove a negative?! If they get to you, if you break...it's all over.

NORA: Funny. If it's so important what I do...

JACK: Don't say I treat you like it's not!

NORA: ...why didn't you warn me this was coming? It would have been considerate. Not to mention prudent. How could you leave me exposed?!

JACK: *(Staring at her, choked)* Nora...

NORA: Because Nora's tough. She can take it. Why not? Every day there's another blow, and I take it. You did this crime; I did that—every illegal, unthinkable, impeachable thing on the books. But this girl is different. You knew this would flatten me. I'd be devastated. Because how could any woman stand up—when the whole *planet* knows she has a faithless husband—and smile!

JACK: *(Pause. Quiet)* I thought you'd know it was a lie.

NORA: How would I know? Because you swore it?

JACK: *(Gets up swiftly, angry)* Excuse me. I have work to do.

NORA: Don't you dare.

JACK: I've got to finish the speech.

NORA: Don't you *dare* fling your "job" at me!

JACK: *(Stopping, breathless —)* This is destructive. And meaningless.

NORA: That I should question you?

JACK: In the long run, none of it has the least importance. So, excuse me, and I'll get back to what does.

(JACK *leaves.* NORA *stands alone.*)

(JACK *passes* RUSS *and* KAT, *who stand to attention, as he continues swiftly into his room.*)

KAT: Oh my god...

(KAT *hurries in to* NORA, *who stares at her.*)

NORA: Call my driver.

KAT: Where are you going?

NORA: Don't argue. I'm not under arrest. I'm going home. *(Begins packing)*

KAT: The President needs you here.

NORA: Does he?

KAT: What happened?

(NORA *intakes air sharply, faces* KAT.)

NORA: Don't get in my way, Kat. I'm about to disintegrate.

KAT: No you aren't. Just take it easy.

NORA: How?!

KAT: Sit down. Breathe.

NORA: Sure.

KAT: Just do it. We're going to think. Reason it out.

NORA: *(Edgy laugh)* Reason?

KAT: You've got to. You're going mad because you can't get hold of it.

NORA: Well it's too much.

KAT: Think, Nora—what his enemies have to gain by creating this story. Then—consider what Jack has to lose if he's done what they say. Which is more likely to be true?

NORA: I should decide based on probability?

KAT: Until you believe him, or them, probability is all you have.

NORA: I don't want to talk about this.

KAT: Yes you do. You have to.

NORA: I want to get out of here.

KAT: Nora, I'm here, too. We're all in this. It could be the worst yet. But have I ever let you down?

(NORA *shakes her head, numb.*)

KAT: Let me help you. Do me the favor.

NORA: Kat, I just...

KAT: Sit.

NORA: I think I'm.... I better lie down.

KAT: Yes. Please. I'll be right....

(KAT *quickly, breathlessly, slips out into the middle office.*)

(KAT *stands staring at* RUSS.)

KAT: Help.

RUSS: *(On phone)* Is that all? Got it. *(Hangs up)* What?

KAT: Dam's gonna burst. I don't think I can hold her.

RUSS: You have to! You don't know what's...

(*Full of his own problems,* RUSS *is on his way into* JACK's *space.*)

KAT: Find out what's wrong; find out what he said to her, Russ. She's going to leave.

RUSS: Jesus.

(RUSS *stands staring at* KAT *as she disappears back into* NORA's *space. Then* RUSS *turns, and moves into* JACK's *space.*)

(JACK *is deep at work, writing his speech.* RUSS *stands in the door.* JACK *senses him and lifts his head, dazed.*)

RUSS: Sorry. *(Beat)* How's the speech looking?

JACK: I'm able to work, if that's what you're asking.

RUSS: Did Nora...?

JACK: Ask her.

RUSS: She won't....

JACK: I've got nothing to say!

(RUSS *stands stymied.*)

JACK: What else? The deluge?

RUSS: *(Uneasy)* Looks like...the lull was momentary. Containing this is like trying to press steam into a bottle—these accusations....

JACK: All without a source?

RUSS: No one will go on record. And accusations keep coming. But no Democrats—even Republicans won't comment.

JACK: Missing a chance to swipe at me?

RUSS: It's like no one wants to be associated. Like it's too hot to touch.

JACK: *(Sighing)* Well, well.

RUSS: I'm worried.

JACK: 'Course you are. When everyone says you're a fool to believe me, what are you supposed to think?

RUSS: I think you've got to be clearer.

JACK: Publish a diary of private thoughts? I eat for them, breathe for them, shit for them—like some highly integrated public service machine! What more do they want?!

RUSS: I don't know, Sir.

JACK: *(Flaring)* Dammit!

RUSS: I don't know, Jack.

JACK: It's as though the more I live for them, the more they own me. And it's harder and harder to breathe!

RUSS: They vote for you—they get a say. You embrace them, before you know it, they begin to identify; then, boom, they're locked on, and you're them. And they don't want you doing anything *they'd* be embarrassed to admit to.

JACK: When a man has no life of his own, is he human?

RUSS: *(Beat)* I've spoken to David. He agrees you were right.

JACK: *(Angry)* Right?! *(Pause, then, tight—)* You mean I can say what I want, tell them what I think?

RUSS: *(Carefully)* Not just anything. David will still restrict what you discuss, but he agrees that a more aggressive tone is needed.

JACK: *(Flat)* Great.

RUSS: You don't sound relieved.

JACK: Should I be? This makes it all better?

RUSS: It's certainly a step in the right....

JACK: Well, I won't make another statement, Russ.

RUSS: *(Stunned)* You won't...

JACK: I said what I have to say.

RUSS: *(Scared)* Jack...

JACK: I told them I didn't do it. If they choose not to believe me...

RUSS: You're going to cut off your nose to spite your face?!

JACK: *(Going back to work)* I have nothing to say.

RUSS: *(Pause)* Is this about Nora? *(Pause)* Jack?

JACK: Nora can say what she likes.

RUSS: Jack.

JACK: *(Pause)* She's not with me, Russ.

RUSS: I know, but you've got to understand....

JACK: Until she is...I make no statement.

(RUSS *stares at* JACK, *stunned by the impossible weight.*)

END OF ACT ONE

ACT TWO

(NORA *stands facing* KAT *at a distance No time has passed.*)

KAT: *(Silence)* Please. You can fall apart with me. Just...rest here.

NORA: *(Frozen)* Is my car ready?

KAT: I can keep everyone away. It's safer, Nora. Please.

NORA: I need....

KAT: You need quiet.

NORA: *(Agitated)* No. Because when it gets quiet, I want to pray. And I can't, Kat. Something's terribly wrong. I can't pray.

KAT: *(Taking hold of* NORA*)* Shhh. First you need to breathe...slow...that's it.

(NORA *inhales deeply, yields, collapses on the lounge.* KAT *begins by stroking her, then will massage her as they talk.*)

NORA: *(Pause)* How could he...?

KAT: He couldn't. But that's what we have to sort through. Because we're forced to. You do know how easily this could be concocted?

NORA: And I'm a duck in a shoot.

KAT: Goes with the territory. And sexual heat in a power center is a weapon of mass destruction.

NORA: Got that right.

KAT: And who's the prime target? Of men in the world ripe for ambush, who's the focus of more female dreams than Jack? Forget morality—just raw female pheromones. He's the number-one conquest in the universe. Who are you to stand in the way?

NORA: Yeah, who?

KAT: You're delicate, private, even shy....

NORA: Shy?!

KAT: Yes, shy. It's painful for you to get out and fight. But he's yours, Nora. That makes you top gun. So there'll always be challengers.

NORA: *(Groaning)* It's so easy for him.

KAT: He mixes; he loves it—like warm water, he flows. And do you think there's some gentle*woman's* agreement because he's married? Think again. All women need to attract all men, like all men want to conquer all women.

NORA: *That's* not true.

KAT: Oh, yes—wherever you have sexual bodies, you have vibrations that have to be harmonized. It's fun, it's life.

NORA: Sure.

KAT: Nora, you do it. You feel your effect when you enter a roomful of men. And you have ways of enhancing that effect. Of stroking them, of appealing to their maleness.

NORA: What does that have to do with...

KAT: It's life. For any female, it's a way of connecting, of redressing power, of assuring her appeal. But the young one is dangerous game—the novice. Because her budding self-esteem feeds on attracting everything in pants, the more powerful the better. Secure that high-powered sperm! That's her mission, and she's at her peak of appeal, but she's completely untested, and she'll try anything. She has no conscience, and no fear of reprisals, because she has nothing yet to lose. She's just scraping off her baby fat. Who can hold her responsible? So the grown man bears it all. *He* has something to lose—a wife, a family, a job, his mind. He should know better.

NORA: Interns. Ever seen an ugly one?

KAT: Negative. America's brightest and best.

NORA: And most ambitious.

KAT: Energetic, ecstatic to be here...

NORA: I should hope so.

KAT: ...and they all, without exception, adore him.

NORA: Piece a cake.

KAT: And to be noticed, to get a personal touch of him? They're wild for it; if they achieve it, even for a second, they soar above their peers, into heaven.

NORA: The King dispenseth his glory.

KAT: As Queen, you're the preventor, prohibitor, denyer.

NORA: How attractive.

KAT: Even if he wants to be faithful, there are heavy guns amassed against it.

NORA: And God help me if I look militant.

KAT: Nora, if you could see through his eyes for one day, sniff what's shoved at him, feel, even a smidgen of the male urge to get up and oblige all that desire, you'd consider yourself lucky he has so much to lose.

NORA: So, another requisite for my office? I have to feel "the male urge"?

KAT: It's nothing like ours.

NORA: Speak for yourself.

KAT: I am.

NORA: You don't know what sex means to me. Why are we having this discussion?!

KAT: I'll bet the difference is biological—something to do with penetration versus reception.

NORA: Will you stop?!

KAT: No, we've got to bring the guy *inside*; that makes us vulnerable, so we want love.

NORA: *(Pounces) That* is not biological.

KAT: All I'm saying is a man's sexual behavior has nothing to do with his goodness, or nobility, or spirituality....

NORA: And a woman's does?

KAT: ...or brains.

NORA: Promiscuous women are pariahs!

KAT: Because they're out of control.

NORA: Of men?

KAT: Who *teach* us "monogamy equals love", when as a matter of fact...

NORA: So a monogamous man is in the control of women?

KAT: Well, some species...

NORA: ...choose monogamy. Presumbly because it benefits the young.

KAT: There are other benefits.

NORA: Like longevity, security...

KAT: Peace, health...

NORA: Forget it. I want to go back to the bush.

KAT: Where we make off with any appealing stud.

NORA: Forget "monogamy equals love".

KAT: *(With a twinkle)* Well...suspend it.

NORA: *(Catching the hilarity)* In the event of bush encounters.

KAT: Equal time in the bush!

(They're laughing. NORA laughs hard, until she cries.)

NORA: *(Laughing and crying)* "So darling, tell me she's only a bush encounter."

KAT: *(Holds her)* Cry, baby.

(Pause, until both are breathing quietly, drifting. Then—)

NORA: It's probably better not to love.

KAT: Do you think it's easier for a man?

NORA: Maybe not.

KAT: Women expect betrayal.

NORA: That's cynical.

KAT: No. That's why it's more devastating for a man to lose his woman, than vice-versa.

NORA: *(Distant)* He'd go mad.

KAT: You know, the French have it all over us.

NORA: Kat...

KAT: A Frenchwoman measures her husband's love by how well he treats her, not by whether he's faithful. And he has to accept her lovers. The sexes can't exploit each other's trust, because they're equal.

NORA: What's this about, Kat? How natural infidelity is, if I'd only relax? Have you *ever* been in love?

KAT: *(Stares at* NORA, *hurt. Finally—)* I'm trying to help.

NORA: Yeah. *(Pause)* If it's true, there's no way I can go on with him. *(Beat)* But—what scares me nearly as much—if it isn't true, how will we ever get past it?

KAT: You have to. Your marriage is not just yours.

NORA: *(Short laugh)* It's a public trust? *(Beat)* And if it's a lie?

KAT: You believe in him, or you wouldn't be here. Unless your ambition would keep you from...

NORA: Don't go there!

KAT: Nora, I know why you're here. You have to know, too.

NORA: This is my life! I won't be the butt of a farce!

KAT: Did he tell you it's true?

NORA: What can he say? He has to deny it.

KAT: To you?

NORA: He doesn't want to hurt me. Or he's afraid I'll leave him. Or he thinks I'll fight better if I think he's innocent. Any way you cut it, if he confesses, he's finished. And for what? It turns everything he's done into a pathetic tragi-comedy. Overnight. His glory's built on sleaze. A dickhead is leading the world!

*(*KAT *stares. Then, strangely, moved to tears, she chokes—)*

KAT: Why can't you trust him?

NORA: Do you?

KAT: *(Upset)* Why doesn't anybody consider the source?! Why is the premise that a bimbo lied *less* likely than that the President has risked everything?

NORA: You're telling me Laurinda isn't worth it?

KAT: That's beneath you! She's nothing. Less than nothing!

NORA: Oh? What happened to your "it's only the male urge"?

KAT: That this twit could cause so much damage is obscene!

NORA: You love him.

KAT: *(Stopped cold, beat)* Of course I do. *(Beat)* Nora. There is no doubt he loves you, honors you, before anyone on earth. And in this case, the country depends upon it.

NORA: On love? Very romantic. *(Pause)* You know, there's a kind of challenger you didn't describe, Kat. The one who, perhaps puritanically, will seduce a man's mind, or his spirit. She feels it's the ultimate conquest. In fact, she sneers at women he sleeps with. Know what I mean?

KAT: I suppose.

NORA: Which should I fear more?

KAT: You've nothing to fear.

NORA: You mean he's never slept with you?

KAT: Stop this!

NORA: That's not the right answer. You're supposed to lie. I don't have to keep tabs on my husband's libido. You do it for me.

KAT: I won't dignify this. You've got enough trouble.

NORA: Is there someone he hasn't slept with?

KAT: Because he acts that way? Because women wish he would? Because he makes women feel desirable, because he mentors them....

NORA: *(Laughing)* "Mentors"!?

KAT: You were happy enough to be the one he chose.

NORA: He chose me because I could do the most for him!

KAT: And now you want out of the job?

NORA: You can have it! *(Beat)* Or would you rather I stayed? Like a paper tiger, stuffed with shreds—of all the statements, documents, files labeled "LIES." *(Breaks down crying)* Well I can't. I just don't care any more. You've got him now. Do your worst.

(NORA *glares at* KAT, *who backs away toward the door.*)

(KAT, *shattered and shaking, outside* NORA's *door, stumbles into* RUSS, *who's on his way to see* NORA *with a draft of the speech in his hand.*)

RUSS: Jack's going ahead with a second draft of the speech, but I'd like to review this with Nora.

KAT: Don't even think about it. She's going to leave.

RUSS: She can't.

KAT: No?

RUSS: What's wrong with you?

KAT: Slight disaster.

RUSS: Did you talk to her?

KAT: I, uh...tried.

RUSS: What happened?

(KAT *looks at* RUSS, *but can't answer.*)

RUSS: *(Alarmed)* Kat?

KAT: She won't avoid it, Russ.

Russ She's got to grow up. There's too much riding on this.

KAT: You try.

RUSS: Me? *(Nervous, he stares at the manuscript, flipping pages.)*

KAT: Talk to her. She doesn't...trust me.

RUSS: What?!

KAT: *(Rushing)* And she knows you have her interests at heart.

RUSS: What if they don't coincide with the interests of the country?

KAT: *(Collapsing in a chair)* Then tell her that. But you've got to confront "did he or didn't he?"

RUSS: That's not the way to reach her.

KAT: She called him a dickhead, Russ!

RUSS: Oh.

KAT: And isn't he both? A giant, and also a dickhead. How can we spin that? It's too trashy to be a tragic flaw.

RUSS: And you wonder why Nora won't listen to you?

(KAT, *punch-drunk and fighting tears, staggers up into what will become a rampage.*)

KAT: Face it, Russ. Adoration flows to him. All of us fantasize wall-to-wall gratification. If he can actually get his, why the hell not?

RUSS: Because that's asking to be struck down!

KAT: Maybe he wants to be struck. It's his dark side—despising himself, daring God, testing his power.

RUSS: That's sick.

KAT: But he's king. Zeus did it. Are you sure Jehovah wouldn't? How high do we rate—as prerequisite for office, that a leader be faithful to women?!

RUSS: Calm down, Kat, I'm on your side.

KAT: This P C crapola has got a lot to answer for.

RUSS: Now wait a minute. It isn't only women who...

KAT: Who what?—Are so twisted as to think sex is a character issue? Who else does? Jealous men?

RUSS: Are you saying this is payback? "Female outrage topples the macho code"?

KAT: *(Punch-drunk giggles)* My god—how to shrivel your enemies' balls! To attack Jack on womanizing, they have to break their macho code of silence. Expect schizoid backpedaling, my friend. As in campaign finance reform—the golden egg must never hatch.

RUSS: What has got into you?

KAT: Are we any different, given his chance? You show me a secretary that doesn't fantasize about her boss. Even a repulsive boss. Woman serving man gets fantasies of doing him *full* service. Just as he fantasizes getting it.

RUSS: My god. Down, Kat.

KAT: It's the slave-promoted-to-intimacy fantasy. Because in desire, the power *shifts! (Winding down, she stumbles to sitting, breathing hard.)*

RUSS: And vice versa? A man with a female boss?

KAT: Probably...

RUSS: What did Nora say to you?!

KAT: *(Ignoring him)* ...but the public's catching on to this, because in reality, no one cares! Sex *has* no importance relative to the economy, safety, and leadership. Kings are too valuable.

(RUSS *stares at* KAT *until he's sure she's finished. Then darkly—*)

RUSS: And where does his wife come into it?

KAT: The wife is reality. The secretary is.... Well, you just hope there's a good grip on reality.

RUSS: Yes.

KAT: *(Pause)* Will you level with me? *(Pause)* Laurinda Wells.

RUSS: *(Pause)* She was a problem. *(He looks at the speech again—glum, intense.)*

KAT: You do remember.

RUSS: Vaguely. She was bright-faced, always popping up in odd places.

KAT: Why does everyone assume it's his doing?

RUSS: Where's the line? You know how to draw it?

KAT: How to spot a predator in a smiling face? How to say no, and risk offending? I wonder every time I date.

RUSS: Men don't know either. Whatever encouragement Jack gave or didn't give, she became obsessed.

KAT: God. This is your line now?

RUSS: He had to get rid of her, because she wouldn't stay away, kept finding excuses to stay in touch.

KAT: So, let her down easy. Avoid a scandal, even of appearances.

RUSS: Especially of appearances.

KAT: That's what you have?

RUSS: At best.

KAT: At best?

RUSS: Who knows? *(Bitter)* As you kindly point out, someone like Jack takes privileges.

KAT: With someone like Nora?

RUSS: *(Stares at* KAT, *then suddenly tough—)* You jumped on me for pushing Nora. Well, let me tell you, you don't ask nearly enough of her. For all your wit, efficiency, effectiveness, you're still "service" personnel. You set the scene, you stay behind, you don't take frontline hits.

KAT: *(Insulted)* And you?

RUSS: That's right. Me too. But I know what she's made of. *(Rises, furious)* So don't get me started.

KAT: All right, all right...

RUSS: *(Trying to control himself)* How is she?

KAT: *(Wary of his mood)* She's...pretty much wrecked.

RUSS: And I have to watch. God, Kat, do you even begin to know who she is? What he's wasted here?!

(KAT, *frightened, stares at* RUSS, *who holds his rage quietly—)*

RUSS: Do you realize...Nora could have been President. There was a brief moment, during the honeymoon, when the public began to realize her stature, and they said so. They put more faith in her than in him.

KAT: Well, she was easier to like. But then she got squashed.

RUSS: Not right away.

KAT: They didn't let her partner him.

RUSS: But she did. Remember when she went to Congress? They were astonished, in awe of her. A woman was *leading*. And not only was she leading, she was right. And not only did they feel she was right, but it felt *good*!

KAT: So they destroyed her?

RUSS: They had to! Imagine the dynasty inherent in her. When he was no longer President, she could run. Who cares if it was retro—with her hoisted on his shoulders—it was working. He was paving the way for women to rule. She had to be stopped.

KAT: Well she is. Squeezed firmly back in the wife hole.

RUSS: And feared.

KAT: Kill the prophet. Makes sense. She was fearless; it backfired—now she's the fall guy.

RUSS: I could kill him!

(KAT *stares at* RUSS, *astonished.*)

KAT: Russ, take it easy. Let's just...protect her.

Russ How? She's in public. She can't have feelings.

KAT: You think he did it?

RUSS: What the hell do I care?!

(RUSS *glares at* KAT, *then realizes how alarmed she is, and calms himself.*)

RUSS: All right. All right, I'll talk to her. (*He strides away.*)

KAT: Wait, Russ. Be careful you don't...

(*But she sees* RUSS *knocking at* JACK's *door, and stops. A phone rings.*)

KAT: That may be her car.

RUSS: Don't let anybody go.

(KAT *picks up the phone.* RUSS *knocks.* JACK, *deep in his writing, hears the knock, gets swiftly to his feet, expecting* NORA.)

JACK: Yes!

RUSS: Sorry, it's me.

JACK: Yes?

RUSS: I couldn't give this to Nora, so I just put my comments in the margin.

JACK: Why couldn't you?

RUSS: She's sleeping.

JACK: *(Beat, looking at* RUSS*)* No, she's not. *(Turns back to his work)* You shouldn't lie, Russ. You're not much good at it.

RUSS: Doggone. You'd think, with all the practice I get...

JACK: What happened.

RUSS: Kat's done all she could. She failed.

JACK: Then you talk to her.

RUSS: You might not like what I say to her.

(JACK *stops to look at* RUSS.)

JACK: Oh?

RUSS: You've betrayed her.

JACK: What!

RUSS: You may not think so. You figure whatever you've done has no effect on your feelings for her, so why hurt her by trying to explain.

JACK: I *did* explain.

RUSS: You figure, she knows how much you love her, so why—given all she has with you—would she risk upsetting the cart?

JACK: What do you know about betrayal?! Betrayal is overlooking her seven reasons why I should veto some bill, or thinking she's gained weight, or an argument about Jody. Betrayal is *any* breach that creates a gap in trust. And there are fewer of those gaps between me and Nora than any two people I know!

RUSS: People make up stories for a reason, Jack. They don't happen from thin air.

JACK: Yes! I attract those stories. I can't help who I am. Would you rather I was you? Should Nora have a man like you?

RUSS: I think Nora can choose for herself.

JACK: Right. *(Beat)* Is there anything else?

RUSS: *(Faces him. Finally—)* No.

JACK: I'm the one Nora wanted, Russ, for better or worse. And you have to admit...I've showed her some good times. *(Grins at* RUSS*)*

RUSS: Damn you!

(JACK *lurches to his feet, to fight. As* RUSS *grabs him,* KAT—)

KAT: Excuse me. David's on line two for you. The heat's up. All the major morning dailies have Laurinda Wells above the fold. He wants you to make an absolute denial. Before the speech.

JACK: Frying pan into the fire—why not? If my wife is "betrayed", if she, of all people, thinks I'm so out of control, so self-destructive! She thinks I don't know every twitch of my nostril is magnified fifty power?!

RUSS: You think this'll help?!

JACK: Tell me why, the more I accomplish, the farther they'll go to bring me down? And let's see. What can they accuse me of that everyone will believe, automatically? Who cares if it's true. It doesn't even have to be credible!

KAT: Calm down, sir.

JACK: Aren't they afraid? If they buy this, they ought to be terrified. Because I'd have to have a death-wish. What kind of misfit is leading the country?

RUSS: *(To* KAT, *irony)* Tell David we'll get back to him.

JACK: How in hell am I supposed to get anything done?!

(KAT *picks up* JACK's *phone and talks to David.)*

JACK: There's no crime been committed; I can't prove someone else did it *instead* of me. Why is this happening?!

RUSS: You tell me.

JACK: What does it mean when I say, categorically, "This did not happen" and people believe it did? That when the consequences of admitting a thing are devastating enough, everyone lies? So I just bet my word, against someone else's, and hope mine weighs more, with no expectation that anyone will actually believe me!

(JACK *faces* RUSS, *who stares at him without flinching.)*

JACK: Or, knowing all the time people will believe *not* what I say, but some vision they create. Still, somewhere, we believe there *is* an absolute answer, don't we—a text of what really happened. But who decides what it is?

KAT: *(Hanging up the phone)* David says you'll be questioned the second you're out the door, no matter the occasion. He wants us to prepare a tough statement.

(JACK *glares at* RUSS, *then suddenly sits, quiet.)*

JACK: No.

KAT: What?

JACK: Russ knows my position.

(KAT *looks at* RUSS. JACK *picks up his pen, acting unconcerned—)*

JACK: Seems you can say anything about anyone these days.

KAT: Well, rarely have so many people had so much to gain by a lie.

JACK: Funny, isn't it. The magic...in what *could* be true. If you can *imagine* it happening, a lie is nearly as good, sometimes better, than a truth. Especially if it's more titillating. In fact, does truth matter, when there's staunch belief in the lie?

(KAT *looks at* RUSS. JACK *goes on writing.*)

KAT: What is his position?

RUSS: No statement without Nora.

KAT: *(Sinking)* Noooo.

JACK: *(Still writing)* She has such a clear soul. She's marvelous, Kat. You can trust her till the sky crumbles. She keeps me honest. *(Looks at* KAT. *Pause)* She can't live without truth.

KAT: That's right.

JACK: I need her with me. If she's not, I don't stand a chance. And, in order to be with me, she has to believe me. There's no other way for her. You and Russ don't need to believe me, to pretend you do. You've got a zillion reasons to defend the appearance of innocence. But if Nora doesn't believe, her soul is offended. And it shows.

(*Silence.* RUSS *turns away, feeling sick.* KAT *takes the weight—*)

KAT: So you want us to make Nora believe you're innocent.

JACK: How do you know I'm not? Why does everyone think they know?!

KAT: Because, Mr President...not knowing is too painful.

(RUSS *puts his hand on* KAT's *shoulder, as they both look at* JACK.)

(NORA—*alone. She's sitting with a book open.*)

NORA: Why can't I talk to you? Oh God, what's wrong with me? Has this hurt gone so deep I can't calm my heart enough to.... I know you'll be there if I only.... Please, I need help here. God, help me! This Bible's no help, let me tell you. *(Reads)* "Then Jacob rose up, and set his sons and his wives upon camels." *Wives*? What's that—different folks, different stro...? Doesn't matter, none of it. It all turns on what I can accept, right? A great love could render sexual faithfulness unimportant, right? If I felt myself so perfectly completed by my love that separation from him was death. *(Pause)* Yes. I know. When we're one, the joy is...so clear, it must be ecstasy. Is it? You know, you must—the floating place, unspeakably tender, where I see, and am, my lover's soul, and both of us angels, both just born. *(Pause)* But how rare are those times? Or how sustainable, when we're loose in the world. If I allow my love to be himself, and love him for whoever he is, instead of demanding he conform to my way of being as a condition of granting my love... Condition. No, that's not right.

(RUSS *enters, quietly.* NORA *turns and looks at him.*)

NORA: I have to consider whether keeping the shell—of everything I thought I had—is worth it—the apparent happiness, security, faith. Can I settle, rather than tear it all out of my heart? Oh, Russell, throwing out a broken dream is the loneliest thing. Because then I'll have nothing.

RUSS: Nora.

NORA: Shhh. I don't want to hear "I told you so."

RUSS: I won't say it.

NORA: No advice?

RUSS: I gave up on that. You'll never leave him.

NORA: Oh oh. Predicting what a woman will do? *(Relaxing a bit)* You know, I've noticed, as time goes by, a sliding scale on "how much I'll take." As a girl, my view was simple black and white—"that's evil, this is good"—but I had to keep redefining my limits based on what reality handed me. Now, some would say I weakened my guidelines, but it did teach me tolerance—which is a good thing. Isn't it?

RUSS: Yes.

NORA: Don't be afraid, Russ. For example—men think of sex quite differently from women. True or false?

RUSS: Nora...

NORA: You can't lie to me, Russ.

RUSS: I...

NORA: That's it. Tell the truth.

RUSS: *(Pause)* I wonder if women think of it at all.

NORA: What?

RUSS: You could, perhaps, go an hour, or a day without?

NORA: Thinking of it? *(Beat)* Yes. Couldn't you?

RUSS: *(Looking at her)* No.

(NORA, *looking at* RUSS, *finally smiles, releasing the tension.*)

NORA: Well. There you are. I've grown a lot from being forced to see through another's eyes. *(Pause)* For example...aren't we supposed to win our mate with love? And hold him. But confinement is counter to life. If I fear competition, and every time there's a skirmish I hold him accountable, I've already lost. If I challenge him, I make myself his parent, and I'm imprisoned—in my own rigidity. That can't be love.

RUSS: Jack didn't do it.

NORA: *(Looks at him, shaken)* Is that for me? Or the press. God, do they know what damage they do? Do they think I need them to point out signs, clues, gossip!

RUSS: Nora, please...

NORA: Oh, Russell, be careful of suspicion. Iago was right. It shrivels love. Deforms it...like acid.

RUSS: *(Choked up, watching her)* I know.

NORA: *(Looks at him, then quickly—)* I can escape. If I stay innocent, unsuspecting... But he should respect me enough not to lie. My pride requires it! And he'll never do something so hard on himself. He's a coward.

RUSS: Nora. *(Catching hold of her)* He didn't do it.

NORA: *(Stares at him)* Good reading. Has the ring of conviction. How do you know?

RUSS: You know yourself. He couldn't live without you.

NORA: That's not an answer. *(She moves away.)*

RUSS: He told me he didn't do it.

(NORA stares at RUSS, deciding.)

RUSS: And I take him at his word.

NORA: "Take him at his word"? What does that mean? It sounds like "I take the position of assuming he's telling the truth" or "because it seems the wisest move, I let him tell me what he *says* is the truth, and I accept it."

RUSS: Nora, don't...

NORA: Why don't you say you *believe* him!

RUSS: I believe him.

NORA: *(Stares at him, then laughs)* No, you don't. *(Beat)* Do you think I can't tell?

RUSS: Oh, Nora.

(RUSS holds out his arms and NORA moves into them, and clings to him, sobbing.)

RUSS: You know they'll say *anything* to tear him down. But he's wildly popular. The people *will not believe* Jack's working against them, even on issues they hate. What can his enemies do? Hit his weak point, sex is easy to believe.

NORA: I know you'd give your life for him, Russ. But not my honor. Please.

RUSS: Nora. Look at it. It's a comedy of lies. *Nobody* can find the truth. When we know we'll never know, what can we do?

NORA: You're killing me!

RUSS: We have to choose. But when our minds have dwelt on every possibility, with no hope of knowing the truth, the possibilities take on the life our mind gives them—and the actual truth recedes.

NORA: What you're saying is, we're going mad.

RUSS: Aren't you afraid of disbelieving him? Have you considered the damage?

NORA: Of course I have! What could be worse? You tell me—to mistrust him if he's telling the truth, or to trust him if he's lying?

RUSS: Oh, Nora. *(Holds her tight)* You'll tear yourself apart. All that matters is what you believe.

NORA: And we'll never know. Like with O J.

RUSS: Sure, like that—everyone hears everything, but we still don't know, and the truth is not as important as what we need to believe. In fact, what we care about most are the meanings—the butchery, the deaths, the rage of O J, the passion of the survivors, or the passion of those who want O J free. We choose to believe whatever we can hang our values on.

NORA: And the President?

RUSS: There's the same rage after the truth, but what do we really care about—an infidelity? Invasion of privacy? Misconduct in the public trust? Political revenge? Voyeurism in the media. Or the fate of the nation. Nora, I'm beginning to see a weird phenomenon. When there is such intimate inquiry, it may be "the truth" will disappear altogether. Because when we look so close, the picture blurs. And if we're human, we're not black and white. Just gray. All gray.

NORA: But there is truth. O J did or did not kill. The President did or did not have sex with an intern.

RUSS: But does it matter? Couldn't this be the farce of our time? That as we slice the human heart thinner and thinner on our home screens, we finally lose it. For the heart cannot ultimately be known. Any more than sex or death can be.

NORA: *(Laugh)* You're priceless, Russ. I wish it was so simple.

RUSS: Nora, when I think of what this has cost you...

NORA: *(Pats him)* You think I chose wrong?

RUSS: *(Looks at her)* I don't know.

NORA: Poor Russell. It's not like I've been baking cookies. I've been number-one advisor to the most powerful man in the world. That's not nuttin', my friend.

RUSS: No.

NORA: And there's Jody. Who else would I want for the father of my son? Damn, if I could have loved someone else, I would have been spared a lot of grief, but...I'm the one who holds him when he cries. *(Pause)* Maybe it's fatal to join with a man? Maybe you can't be both wife and woman. God, I'm sick of being the lightning rod for every strike against my sex, when, look at me—I'm *so* damned conventional! *(Beat)* At least that's over.

RUSS: What?

NORA: You think infidelity doesn't matter, Russ?

RUSS: What's over, Nora?

NORA: Could *you* be unfaithful to me?

RUSS: Nora...

NORA: Answer me.

RUSS: Don't be stupid. Any man that could...

NORA: Nothing gray about you, is there?

RUSS: ...is no man.

NORA: I see.

RUSS: Nora, please don't let this...

NORA: But you're right. Truth used to be easier to find. A husband would lie as long as he could, and then he'd take the consequences. Well. I'd better tell him.

RUSS: Tell him what?

NORA: Dear Russ. *(Kisses him on the cheek)* I have to leave.

RUSS: No. Why?

NORA: Because I've become as bad as the rest of you. I can't believe what my husband tells me. What kind of a wife is that?

(NORA's moving away.)

RUSS: Nora! *(He is alone.)*

(JACK alone. He looks up from writing, seems to talk to himself, but it's God he's addressing.)

JACK: Is this it then? All right. What you will. Let it come down. I can't ask for mercy—I deserve worse; I'm an asinine, arrogant fool! But you've been with me, haven't you...every day, even the worst, and you know my sins, so why are you here? And you are. Again and again, a challenge comes—to safety, to peace—demanding a terrible gamble; I ask for help, you give me strength, and when I place that strength at risk, you let me win. And millions, millions win with me. Now if I stop, give in, refuse to fight, what then? Will I fall? From such a height. And shatter? Yes, you'll fall, you obscene, reckless, son of a bitch! *(Rage to weeping)* That's all right; it's all right. I have to pay. I know. And I can't fear...whatever comes now. But for them, the people? And her? Oh God, please, don't hurt her more! Don't let my obscenity destroy her. Have mercy on her. Please! Please help her. Give her your hand. Don't let us weary of our walk...too soon. Please, not too soon.

(NORA *stands at* JACK's *entrance; he senses her there, and quickly rises to face her—*)

JACK: Nora.

(*Once facing her,* JACK's *unable to speak, so they stand looking at each other. Finally—*)

NORA: You should know—I'm going to go before it's light. So maybe it won't be noticed...right away.

JACK: (*Intense pain*) Nora...

NORA: Don't. (*Beat*) I can't stay here now.

JACK: Yes. (*Looking at her in stillness. Pause*) All right.

NORA: You all right?

JACK: Sure. (*Pause*) Be careful, O K?

(*They continue to face each other, as though unable to turn away.*)

NORA: Sure. (*Beat*) Anything I should know?

JACK: (*Small laugh*) Before it's on C N N?

NORA: These shocks don't help.

JACK: I know. I'm sorry.

NORA: Yeah. Me too. (*Turning to leave*)

JACK: I'd just.... I've been reworking the opening, and I wish you could.... Before you go, just...

NORA: (*Not wanting to go, not wanting to stay—stuck*) Sure. (*Beat*) Show me.

JACK: Thanks.

(*He brings her a handful of papers. She holds them, staring, bewildered.*)

JACK: Some light? (*He brings a chair, and a lamp.*)

NORA: (*She sits, still shell-shocked.*) Thanks.

(*She reads and he watches, anxious.*)

NORA: (*Still reading*) It's good. Smooth. Strong.

JACK: The part down there, about....

NORA: ...help you've had from the Republicans? It works.

JACK: Now, what you said about working mothers—the way you said it....

NORA: You've got it. Right here. That's it.

JACK: What I don't know is—this last big section, before the end, right here—I feel like doing it. It's what I want to be able to say, but...

NORA: You have to.

JACK: ...they won't know where I'm going, where I'm trying to... It's so out of line from the business of...

NORA: But it's the future. It's exactly where we're going. Paint it! It's just that no one does. Not all together like this, so we can project our minds, our hopes, toward something no one can imagine, but someone can point us to. No one expects from a government, or a politician, such a.... *(She's moved, catches her breath)*

JACK: They won't know what to think. It's not like a proposal they can applaud.

NORA: Because no one has said it, not in public, to all the people. It's a vision! Do you know what that's worth? You have to. Who else should bring it to them!

(NORA's weeping. JACK embraces her, fighting his tears.)

JACK: I'm so sorry you have to go through this.

NORA: Why is it happening, Jack?

JACK: It's not me, Nora. I didn't do what they say. I swear to you.

(NORA shakes her head, pulls away, in agony.)

JACK: I know how tired that sounds. What can I say? There's nothing else.

(NORA looks at the door, starts to rise, but he holds her hand.)

JACK: I did befriend Laurinda Wells, and did not discourage her...at first. And, I did—what you'd call—flirt with her.

(NORA's taking heaving breaths, but it doesn't help. She's overwhelmed by nausea.)

JACK: But I didn't mean anything by it. God, how cheap that sounds! I don't know what else to say. She thought it did mean something, and started crossing the line, and when it got...excessive, I had to ask Milton to help her to a "promotion" elsewhere. I suppose when Laurinda felt the barriers go up, she cracked. So yes, I should have known there'd be trouble, and I should have warned you then. But I felt I was to blame, and I knew how it would hurt you, and God, Nora, you know what you mean to me. Don't go. Please don't.

NORA: Jack, I can't....

JACK: I know, I know. I don't have the right.

NORA: I've already been in a spot where I had to stop caring what you did—in order to respect myself. I can't go there again.

JACK: Am I going to be on trial my whole life?! When can I be assumed innocent!

NORA: That's not up to me!

JACK: Then who?!

(RUSS *opens the door. They're both stunned by the interruption.*)

RUSS: Excuse me. I'm very sorry, but....

JACK: It had better be good.

RUSS: The west coast late news had Charley on.

(KAT *is edging in behind* RUSS.)

JACK: Why? He's not....

RUSS: He's no longer security advisor, but he's considered your close friend.

JACK: So?

RUSS: He said he expects the story is true.

JACK: My god...!

(NORA *sinks into a chair.*)

RUSS: And that if it is, you should resign.

JACK: What?!

RUSS: He's Charley. He runs off at the mouth.

KAT: But it's set off an avalanche.

RUSS: The morning lead, everywhere, is "resign." And you can bet the next word will be "impeach."

NORA: No...

KAT: It can't hold. No one wants that.

NORA: But they'll panic. How could you let it go so far? What will this do to the country?! Why haven't you stopped it?

RUSS: We can't control the press.

NORA: He could speak to the people. He could be forthright. He could step out from behind this legalese, and simply tell them the truth. Except, I forgot, Russ. You don't think the truth matters!

RUSS: They've already decided what to believe. They've made it up. Just like you have, Nora!

(*Stunned, they all stare at* RUSS. *Then—*)

NORA: Who's going to wake up to this, and smile. Mr and Mrs Shopkeeper? Mr and Mrs Teacher, Farmer, Cop, Street-cleaner? Their president's self-destructing? This'll send the country into shock. What can they trust? He's brought them to the peak of believing in themselves and their future. We're happier and more optimistic than we've been for decades, finally regaining our self-respect. Has he insanely jeopardized all this? For what? Because he's afraid of his sexual misconduct? He thinks he's cornered. He's beating himself out of guilt? He doesn't get to do that!

KAT: Nora, please...

JACK: *(Riveted on* NORA*)* Get out of here—Kat, Russ. Leave me alone. With my wife.

(NORA *glares at* JACK, *breathing hard.*)

(KAT *and* RUSS *back out. The lights go with them.*)

KAT: Jesus, Mary and Joseph...

RUSS: Come on. Move.

KAT: I can't. I can't. What's going to happen?

RUSS: Take a breath. Nothing yet.

KAT: *(Pause)* This is not real.

RUSS: Right. That's right.

KAT: This is not happening.

RUSS: *(Starts to laugh)* Because it can't. Because we can't take it.

KAT: So it won't?

RUSS: We won't let it.

KAT: Get a grip, Russell. Nora's right about what this will do. And here we are standing in the middle of it.

RUSS: No. Here's what goes on: people in stress report events that happened, or could have happened. And if these reports harm other people, those other people counter them—with denials, or another version, offered as the "real" truth.

KAT: And if, as in this case, we fear the truth...?

RUSS: We may choose to alter the consequences, deny its importance, in order to diffuse its power to hurt us. So, do we compromise our values, give up our principles? Or do we acknowledge that our principles were unrealistic or hypocritical. Because a rule for social behavior has been violated by someone too important to condemn for it.

KAT: Wrong. No one would *care* if he weren't important.

RUSS: But if he were dispensible, he'd be dispensed.

KAT: And he can be. If no one believes the President, how can he stay President?

RUSS: Magic.

KAT: Good luck.

RUSS: I'm telling you, a giant disconnect is taking place. Unless he folds, the people are going to save him....

KAT: Oh, good.

RUSS: ...because he's in love with them.

KAT: Yeah. Locked in wooing gear.

RUSS: With his giant ambition. Have you ever seen any man's ambition so married to the future of his people, *all* his people?

KAT: He's a hopeless idealist, Russ.

RUSS: But with brains. And the nerve to act.

KAT: And pride.

RUSS: Yes, he's arrogant.

KAT: He's overweaning, devious...

RUSS: Lustful.

KAT: ...clumsy, naive...

RUSS: But he's married to them. They won't ever give him up. No matter what he does with his dick, his soul is theirs—and he'll never be unfaithful.

KAT: Have you informed his wife?

(*Lights switch from* KAT *and* RUSS *to* JACK *and* NORA, *as they were.*)

NORA: Why is this happening, Jack? Did you let it go to this insane length to punish me?

JACK: Punish you?

NORA: Because I don't believe you?

JACK: I didn't ask for this.

NORA: Or are you acting this way out of guilt? You want to be drummed out of office?

JACK: No!

NORA: You can spin better than this. You're risking the country. How can you? Damn you! Why did you let them trust you?

JACK: But they don't.

NORA: So you're taking your marbles home? You have responsibility here!

JACK: Didn't know you cared.

NORA: Don't you dare!

JACK: Excuse me.

NORA: Oh, Christ. Just tell me what you're pulling.

JACK: You think I can control events?

NORA: I know you're risking impeachment.

JACK: I had no idea this would...

NORA: No, but you're testing. You want to taste the danger—"What if I should topple?" What about the people?

JACK: No one trusts me!

NORA: They trust that you're going to lead! Not abdicate. Who do you think they want in your place? You've made yourself everything to them. Just like to me. Damn you!

JACK: I have to bear my sins. Why can't you?!

(NORA *stares at* JACK, *backs off, stricken by his implication.*)

NORA: Maybe your sins are what they believe in—seeing all you've accomplished in spite of your mistakes lets them think *they* have a chance, even though they're human. Like you.

JACK: Nora...

NORA: *(Avoiding him)* Probably it's what they love most. About you.

JACK: And you?

NORA: It's their own promise you hold up to the people—and they believe, because the more they believe, the more real their promise *becomes.*

JACK: And you?

NORA: I have my own problems.

JACK: You're light in my path, Nora. Stay with me.

NORA: Don't...

JACK: God lets me lead. You're meant to lead me.

NORA: Damn you. You turn it on, no matter what. Make love to everyone. But I'm immune. All right? You can spare me.

JACK: Nora, I'm not...

NORA: Don't even try. I know you—you'll trick, you'll twist, you'll charm, you'll find a way, but not with me, not this time!

JACK: All right, hands off, fair enough. *(Beat. Complete change—)* What do you advise?

NORA: What David says. Stop them! Deny this affair, strongly, without mincing words.

JACK: Without you believing me?

NORA: You're angry about this, aren't you?

JACK: *(Calm)* You have Never. Seen me. So angry.

NORA: Then you've got to tell them what you think.

JACK: I'll do it. *(Beat)* If you're with me.

NORA: *(Stunned pause)* You can't do this to me.

JACK: Don't leave.

NORA: This is blackmail!

JACK: I'm not asking you to lie.

NORA: Only to give the *impression* of...

JACK: Stay, because you believe me. That's what I need.

NORA: I believe you?! What? That you're telling the truth? That you won't lie to me? I've been there, Jack. And I can't.

JACK: *(Pause, stopped)* You can't. *(Pause)* Then believe my belief.

NORA: What?

JACK: You say that, on this issue, you can't believe what I tell you.

NORA: *(Strangled laugh)* You've got that.

JACK: Then think—what *do* you believe about me. What do you trust?

NORA: That you love our son. That you don't want to hurt me.

JACK: That I want to lead the country well?

NORA: Of course.

JACK: Do you believe I believe in God?

NORA: *(Beat)* That isn't fair.

JACK: Why not?

NORA: It's a trick.

JACK: No. I want the truth. Answer honestly. I can take it. Do you believe... that I believe in God? Or is it just a manipulation I do?

(NORA *twists about, uncomfortable, finally answers—*)

NORA: You believe in God. When you've taken a bad step, I think you are sorry. I think you look to God to help you mend. *(Breathing with difficulty)* I also think...you depend on what God intends for you. You believe God has brought you where you are, and that he has ultimate power over what will become of you.

JACK: That includes whether you stay or I lose you.

NORA: Yes.

JACK: Whatever the cost, to either of us?

NORA: Yes.

JACK: Then—how will the choice be made?

NORA: I...have to decide...what's right for me.

JACK: Have you made your choice already?

NORA: *(Chokes, from holding back tears)* You're torturing me.

JACK: No. I'm fighting for my life.

NORA: And you can't lose.

JACK: If God's with me.

NORA: Jesus, Jack!

JACK: *(Quickly)* I know you've reasons from the past for not trusting me, Nora. But all I ask you to do...is believe in my belief.

NORA: *(Pressed)* That...

JACK: ...that I commit my life....

NORA: Jack...

JACK: ...and my love...to his service.

(NORA *stares at him. Pause*)

JACK: And ask you to join me. *(Pause)* Do you believe...these things?

(JACK *puts out his hand. It's a trick, but it's true.* NORA *wants to be angry, but can't, any more than she can deny him. Slowly, her hand raises to hold his. Band strikes up. Then they turn together, and walk upstage, toward the flash bulbs.*)

END OF PLAY

IN A KINGDOM BY THE SEA

PRODUCTION HISTORY

National Theater Colony, 1990
Circle Repertory Reading, New York, 1991
Playwrights Theater of New Jersey, 1992

CUNY Grad Center, Ralph Bunche Institute, New York, 15 April 1992, produced by Paula Hajar, Associate Producer, Brenda Murad.

SAMI	Theodore Bikel
HOGAN	Richard Poe
LAUREL	Jordan Baker
TOMBO	Curt Hostetter
SHARIF, OPS OFFICER	John Camera
HAJJ, RAYMOND	Tom Spackman
GABE	David Rainey
Narrator	Michael Haney
Director	Richard Edelman
Sound engineer	Phil Lee
Lighting engineer	Ann-Marie Brady
Production stage manager	Tom Dale Keever
Assistant stage manager	Joanna May

CHARACTERS

TOMBO, *Sergeant Thomas Bohanna, Irish, about 30, on his fourth tour in "the Lebanon," laid back, witty, practical, except that he wishes he were a poet.*

GABE, *Corporal Gabriel Mataitini, Fijian, early 20's, a first-timer, strong, with quiet carefulness of the unworldly and proud. Idealistic, and sweet as island honey.*

HOGAN, *Lt Col William Hogan (Hogie), an American Marine, 40's. Hearty, wise-cracking, a bit bigger than life. The short guy, who makes his way by capturing everyone's heart and attention—brash, driven, covering deep emotion, fiercely devoted.*

SAMI *(SAH-mee), Samir Kemal, Turk, late 40's+. An elegant-slob, that is, an utterly unconcerned sophisticate, wise as Father Time, who's given his life to rugged world service.*

LAUREL, *Laurel Marie Maitland, American, 14 to 40's. Exuberant, funny, tender, the unconsciously popular. Endlessly stumbling over herself, but irrepressibly triumphant, she expects life to fight her and give in.*

SHARIF, *Sheik Abdul Majeed Sharif, Lebanese, 30's to 40's, consummate practical diplomat, with one foot solidly in each world— the eastern Muslim and the western secular, he is sharp-eyed, commanding, proud, weary, but absolute.*

HAJJ, *Sheik Abdul Karim Hajj, Lebanese, 30's. Imperious, blazing-eyed savior, with clear, pure intelligence, bound to Muslim tradition and village struggle.*

doubles:

OPS OFFICER *(Operations Officer), late 30's. Commanding, efficient, considerate. (Double with* SHARIF*)*

RAYMOND, *Undersecretary General of the United Nations, British, 50's. Gentle, but giving the impression of great size, does his job with decision and forcefulness, but would be happier in his garden. (Double with* HAJJ*)*

Cast note: females may be cast in U N roles.

SETTING

An open stage, perhaps raked.

A "listening post." Large map of South Lebanon, with pin lights to indicate activity—location of checkpoints, observation posts, squads, movement of vehicles. A table and chairs facing the map, with two-way radios, phones, fax. Chair and desk for SAMI, with keyboard, piled high with clutter.

Clustered, as though suspended—projection screen, monitor, speakers, V C R—the means, simultaneous and fractured, by which we receive our image of events.

Minimum Technology: a screen for projections, and a voice-over mike. Ensemble timing is more important than hardware.

When you begin to love what you passionately misunderstand
the world turns.

ACT ONE

(In level-one reality, we are in the nerve center of UNIFIL—United Nations Interim Force In Lebanon. There is a darting-image feel as two actions play at once. The first begins moments before a kidnapping occurs, and continues to its end. The second is the "presence" of HOGAN, *the kidnap victim, visible only to* SAMI *and the audience; he skips time and space, "tuning in" at will.)*

(Soldiers GABE *and* TOMBO *have their backs to audience as they work at radio communications board, dimly lit only from the board.* GABE *is a Fijian,* TOMBO *is Irish. They wear, with their national uniforms, the sky-blue beret and cravat of United Nations peacekeepers.)*

VOICE-OVER: *(From radio)* Oscar 3 to Delta 1, radio check. Over.

*(*GABE *gets on radio microphone, watching map above his head to coordinate location. The map is a huge version of South Lebanon, delineating UNIFIL's Area of Operations, sectioned into the battalion zones of various donor countries—Irishbatt, Ghanabatt, etc.)*

GABE: Delta 1 here. Where are you now, sir? Over.

VOICE-OVER: We've arrived Tyre, Basini Street five-zero-three. Leaving vehicle. Over.

*(*TOMBO *highlights Tyre. It's outside their Area of Operations.)*

TOMBO: *(Teasingly)* What could they be doing at Amal Headquarters? Visiting Sharif-the-Great, is it?

GABE: *(Ignoring* TOMBO, *into the mike)* I copy...Basini Street five-zero-three. Thank you, Major.

TOMBO: Am I wrong?

VOICE-OVER: Everything quiet in there?

GABE: Like two doves cooing, sir.

TOMBO: Ask him where's the cowboy?

GABE: *(Gestures to* TOMBO *to be quiet)* Ah...Major? Is the Colonel's vehicle there as well?

(Light is coming up on HOGAN, *the cowboy Colonel, somewhere above them—a Lieutenant Colonel in the United States Marine Corps. He is hearty, animated, a bit bigger than life—though not a large man—and proceeding oblivious to them, in another dimension.)*

VOICE-OVER: Pulled in right ahead of me. Hasn't he checked in with you?

GABE: No sir, he hasn't. Thank you, sir. Over. *(To* TOMBO*)* Can I map this? Think I know how.

(TOMBO *nods, and watches* GABE *adjust lights on overhead map board to indicate Oscar 3 and Oscar 1 vehicles' movement into restricted zone and Tyre, then he enters the movement in the log chart.)*

TOMBO: Whheee, the cowboy into the Sheik's lair—da *dum.* But is he ready?

GABE: Why "cowboy"? Leave him alone.

TOMBO: And miss the Yankee Doodle? Colonel Hogan's the best hoot that's happening, lad. Want to bet he'll disappear with some woman in Tyre?

GABE: Bull shit.

TOMBO: Why not?

GABE: Not with a wife named Mary!

> HOGAN: So I'd say to her, Laurel—

(Light full on HOGAN. *He's leaned against a locker, immersed in telling us a story.* GABE *and* TOMBO *are unaware of him.)*

> HOGAN: *(To audience)* You want the key to America? One word? Football. —So I'd say to Laurel, *(suddenly dramatic)* "I can see them coming... straight up the field, barrelling, every single one over three hundred pounds. They'll crush me, punctuate my sweet body with their brutal cleats. Oooh, I'm gonna hurt sooo much. They're gonna kill me tonight!"
> Then she'd hang onto the locker, double over, laughing—
> "Hogie, you un-regenerate, un-mitigated dumbhead! Why do you do it?! Don't go out for team. Be the *mascot.* You could waddle out there just the same." *(Picking up a football)* What could I say to her?

VOICE-OVER: Bravo 7 to Delta 1. Radio check. Over.

(HOGAN *stays lit, waiting for the audience to answer his question, then he speaks again, while the radio laps under him.)*

GABE: Delta 1, what's your location? Over.

> HOGAN: Should I have asked her what she sees? Jumping up, shrieking...her dimpled knees, red as cheeks?

VOICE-OVER: Just cruising the scenic perimeter, two kilometers west of Beaufort Castle.

> HOGAN: What's she see that's so goddammed exciting in some muddy heap sprawled and grunting on the ten-yard line?

GABE: *(Jotting it down)* I copy.

> HOGAN: If she can answer me that, then I'll know why I do it.

(Having made his point, HOGAN *corrects his grip on the football, feints a throw, turns abruptly to lope around the center as radio communications continue.)*

VOICE-OVER: We'll be at OP 34 in about ten minutes. Over.

> HOGAN: But life is like that. Everything gets you ready. And it's not only the girls! It's the moms, the dads, the *alums* for God's sake, and the coach, the whole bald-assed town! They're all on their feet. It's like you're them, and they want you in the goddammed pile— ramming, crunching, dropping those three hundred pounders dead!

TOMBO: *(Leaning in to the mike)* What's the weather out there?

> HOGAN: All you can hope is that somehow you'll get onto the field with all those pads and that gigantic helmet,

VOICE-OVER: Precipitation— Natural or unnatural?

> HOGAN: ...that you won't stumble halfway out and go flat on your face without ever making it to the goddammed pile. Does a woman think of that? *(He slides down the locker, sits.)*

TOMBO: Funny man. Funny.

VOICE-OVER: Here's your report, man: No shelling, and no rain.

GABE: *(Moving Bravo 7 on the map)* Clear that channel. You told me: no chatter.

VOICE-OVER: But considerable sun screen... *(Muffled explosion, shout)*

GABE: Holy fuck! *(Back at mike)* Bravo 7. What happened? Bravo 7? Do you copy? Over.

VOICE-OVER: Na cava oya!

TOMBO: What's that? What's he talking?

GABE: Fijian. *(Into mike)* Bravo 7, report your condition. Over. Tombo, what do I do?

VOICE-OVER: Magai tinamu!!

*(*GABE *and* TOMBO *are dumbfounded for an instant.)*

TOMBO: Can you make it out?

GABE: *(Trying to make it out)* "Mother-ff..." not repeatable. *(Into mike)* Bravo 7, are you all right? Respond in English. Over.

VOICE-OVER: *(Another channel)* Oscar 3 to Delta 1. I'm leaving Tyre. Proceeding south on the coast road.

TOMBO: *(To* GABE*)* Clear that channel, clear the net! And get the Finns. They're closest.

VOICE-OVER: Magai tinamu—shit!

GABE: Bravo 7...

TOMBO: *(Clearly senior, taking over)* Delta 1 to Finnbatt. Emergency on Kafer Kela Road. Do you copy?

> HOGAN: *(Sharply)* The only time I could figure why anyone would do it—and I *told* Laurel—was when you'd get free of the pile... *(He rises to his feet, weaving the ball slowly back and forth.)*

TOMBO: Finnbatt. Do you copy?

> HOGAN: ...I mean really break out, and it was just you, just you, dodging the snags, leaping past all those lunging hulks, finally you, taking off, running wild, soaring down the field, carried on the screaming wave of climax in everyone's throat and chest and thighs. *(Beat)* And that's America! *(He tosses the ball high, then turns to retrieve his Marine hat. The ball is gone.)*

VOICE-OVER: *(Finnish accent)* Finnbatt 4. Ready to copy.

TOMBO: Bravo 7 disabled by an explosion, cause unknown at present, five kilometers south of the castle. Over.

VOICE-OVER: I copy. Stand by. Over.

VOICE-OVER: *(On another channel, panting)* Roadside bomb, must be. Caught left rear...

GABE: *(Into the mike)* Have you injuries?

VOICE-OVER: Don't think...no, Naulu's O K too. Only battered.

(HOGAN squares off, in uniform. Radio exchanges continue, under.)

> HOGAN: Now. You want to know what the hell *I'm* doing in the middle of all this, right? Well, don't worry, I'm gonna tell you. But first...first, I want you to tell *me* something....
>   So go back a minute, O K? The lights come up. Radios going. And up here, you see me, right? A U S Marine. What do you feel? Spit it out, right off the top. You feel— Clean? Country? Pride? Don't give me that bull. Every second one of you hates my guts.

(HOGAN catches sight of SAMI entering, then shoots back at the audience:)

> HOGAN: Why is that?

(SAMI, a middle-aged Turk not in uniform, but casually dressed—jeans, work boots, bush jacket—appears. HOGAN is pleased, and circles, watching closely.)

TOMBO: Hi, hi! It's scintillating Sami, the flying Turk. How was your leave?

(SAMI moves slowly, sighing-in the atmosphere, stops, barely tilts his head towards the soldiers, raises one palm, clicks his tongue, saying:)

SAMI: Kismet. All is Kismet. As Allah wills.

GABE: *(Into mike)* Bravo 7? Finnbatt's coming. Settle in, you're covered.

TOMBO: Good lad, Gabe.

(SAMI *sinks languidly into his considerable chair, beside a desk piled impossibly high with various papers and symbols, including a blue beret. He throws his head back, and shuts out everything.*)

TOMBO: Come on, talk to us, Sami. Give us a tickle. Did you find your harem intact?

VOICE-OVER: *(Finnish accent)* Finnbatt 4 to Delta 1. Over.

GABE: *(Switching to the channel* TOMBO *was on)* Delta 1. Go ahead.

VOICE-OVER: We've dispatched an A P C with an E O D Squad and an armored ambulance to transport the observers back to SwedMedCoy. Over.

TOMBO: Got a bonafide "terrorist" incident proceeding at this moment. Better open your hot wire to New York, Sami. They're dying for this info. It can read "Roadside booby trap, United Nations' vehicle enroute to..."

GABE: Roger. Suspect roadside bomb. Stay tuned. Over.

SAMI: *(Without opening his eyes)* Anyone killed?

TOMBO: No, but there's...

SAMI: No one killed—no one prints it.

(*Silence, soldiers filling logs, then, out of the quiet,* HOGAN *goes on, musing:*)

HOGAN: Most of you don't remember, but there was a time in America when uniform equalled hero. Boys got their manhood in one quick change. Girls shivered with the pleasure of exclusion. Back in the sweet sweet fifties, with everything just getting better and better, and more and more, but then...well, the uniform took a dive, you might say.

But let's get one thing straight. The trouble was not the dream. The American dream was about money. And that'll always be sweet. No. The trouble was the "Ideal." I mean, whoever heard of a country based on the "Principle" that all men are created et cetera, et cetera. And on top of that comes the idiotic idea that we're good or *honest*?! Right away we should have known we were in the shit. I mean, a country *is* because your people belong, not because you "believe" in it.

But what the hell. We had youth, we had money... Except, hold it: What happens when your whole identity is riding on this "ideal" of being good, and it takes you to Nam? Gives you the finger? Involves every damn soldier in genocide?

Well I say, you crack. Who could survive? You crack. And so we did. The uniform was tarnished. The girls didn't catch their breath anymore. Well—when in doubt, stand stronger. That's what I figured. Believe twice as hard. So I stood. And I *believed.* (*He finishes by fixing his focus on* SAMI.) And I wound up here.

SAMI: *(Without moving or opening his eyes)* Sergeant Bohanna?

TOMBO: Yes, Father Sami?

SAMI: Have Finnbatt save a piece of the bomb, bring it in for my museum.

TOMBO: Sure, and I will, Most Reverend Information Officer. I figure it's either S L A, P L O, or I D F. Now, that's a choice of Christian, Muslim, or Jewish terrorists. So how's my neutrality rating?

(HOGAN *laughs loud, then moves to lean over the radio board, listening.*)

GABE: Delta 1 to Oscar 3. Over.

SAMI: Who's the youngster?

TOMBO: Ah, yes...meet Gabriel Matatini. Not the worst Fijian I've met. I'm seriously considering letting him come back tomorrow.

SAMI: First day on the radios?

GABE: Pleased to see you, Mr Kemal. I've driven you a few times. When you made rounds with Colonel Hogan.

VOICE-OVER: Oscar 3 to Delta 1. Over.

GABE: Delta 1. Yes, Major? I show you proceeding south on the coast road. Over.

VOICE-OVER: Delta 1, has Colonel Hogan checked in with you? Over.

GABE: He has not, repeat, not called in. Is he enroute with you, sir?

VOICE-OVER: We left Tyre together, but I don't see him now. I'm going to retrace. Do you copy? Over.

(HOGAN *looks up at the audience, raising a finger....*)

GABE: I copy. You'll reverse direction, hoping to rendezvous with Oscar 1. Thank you, Major. Over.

HOGAN: *(Checking out)* That's it. And I'm off. *(He turns and disappears.)*

TOMBO: Ho hooo. Where's the cowboy Colonel off to now? Sami—have you ever seen the like? Hogan's only two weeks in the top saddle, and already he's taking tea with Sharif the Great, chief of Amal.

SAMI: *(Waving a desultory hand)* So...so, he's taking command.

VOICE-OVER: Oscar 3 to Delta 1. Emergency. Over.

GABE: Jesus. *(Lunges to radio)* Delta 1. Ready to copy.

VOICE-OVER: Colonel Hogan's vehicle is pulled up at the roadside, standing empty.

(*Like a snake coming alert,* SAMI *sits up, motionless.*)

TOMBO: What!

VOICE-OVER: Captain Nilsson is reconnoitering the immediate area on foot. I will standby here. We are unarmed in a restricted zone. Over.

GABE: Jesus, do you think he's....

TOMBO: Calm yourself, Gabriel. We assume, until we find him, that he's missing. Set up a cordon.

GABE: Yes, a cordon. That's...

(SAMI *rises*.)

TOMBO: Find the location. Exactly.

GABE: Yes. *(Into the mike)* Major...Oscar 3? What is your location, sir?

VOICE-OVER: Ras al Ayn. We just passed it. Maybe two kilometers.

TOMBO: *(On a mike)* Delta 1 to Fijibatt. Emergency. Over.

(SAMI *walks slowly downstage*.)

GABE: *(Nervously locating on map)* Two kilometers south of Ras al Ayn. Uh...time. Log time. Major, when did it...when did you...?

VOICE-OVER: Occurred not more than ten minutes ago. Approximately 14:00...

(*This exchange continues under* TOMBO, *who's talking on another channel to Fijibatt*.)

VOICE-OVER: Fijibatt 2 to Delta 1. Ready to copy. Over.

TOMBO: Colonel Hogan's vehicle has been found empty on the coast road in the Tyre pocket approximately two kilometers south of Ras al Ayn. Establish a cordon: Full alert security, for Colonel Hogan, possible abduction underway, at your checkpoints...*(Referring to map)* 1 dash 6, 1 dash 8, and 1 dash 9 Alpha. Also at 1 dash 1 Alpha, 1 dash 1, and 1 dash 23. And...set up a roadblock on the Ayn Bal road where your Area of Operations meets Ghanbatt's. Do you copy? Repeat.

(*Pause*. TOMBO *twists around to look at* SAMI, *while the situation sinks in. The voice-over repeat drones in the background*.)

VOICE-OVER: Maximum level security alert at checkpoints 1-6, 1-8, 1-9 Alpha,1-1 Alpha 1-1, 1-23. Roadblock on Ayn Bal road, edge of our A O. Over.

(*Quiet beat, then* SAMI *explodes*)

SAMI: You bastard! You were alone, weren't you!

(HOGAN *appears, laughing, at his U N reception party, moving toward* SAMI.)

HOGAN: I tell you, Sami, she flew down the hall with more flash and smart-ass than six AK-47's, and then...

(LAUREL *bursts on upstage—spirited, athletic, high school in the fifties—and proceeds toward the locker, tries, with considerable animation, to get it open*.)

SAMI: What's she got to do with...?

HOGAN: She couldn't open her locker, could not do it. Till finally our home-room teacher said "Will *someone* share with Laurel?" And five guys' hands shot up all at once. But me, brand new to the school, I stood up with my moonface and barked: "It's a nasty job, sir, but somebody's got to do it."

(HOGAN *grins like a smart-ass kid, and moves to open the locker. The others have been frozen by* SAMI's *rage.*)

SAMI: *(Snapped with fury)* He was alone, wasn't he!?

TOMBO: Sami...

(*Biting him off,* SAMI *ticks off one order after another—they're sharp, quick, and, like a snake's tongue, do not disturb his essential calm.*)

SAMI: Get your OPS Officer in here. Direct the Major to hunt up witnesses. Call Italair and get choppers off the ground. If he's been abducted there's no reason they'd head straight into Fijibatt's checkpoints, they'll go north through the pocket. He met with Sharif in Tyre? Get Sharif on the line. —Don't stand there wondering what my rank is, my rank is nine hundred years here. And get the OPS Officer!

(TOMBO *runs for the* OPS *(Operations)* OFFICER. GABE *is calling Italair, while* HOGAN *moves into* SAMI's *field of vision, grinning at him.*)

GABE: *(Into the mike)* Delta 1 to Italair. Emergency. Over.

SAMI: *(Without skipping a beat, seeing* HOGAN *in his mind)* Why were you alone, you bastard. Why?!

(LAUREL, *very grateful, is now loading her books into the locker.* HOGAN *plants himself, show-down style, facing* SAMI. *Only* SAMI *can see him.*)

HOGAN: So Laurel moved in, and from then on, laughing or fighting, I took care of her, we were "locker people." And we kept that same locker for four years. We never moved the locker, no matter where our home-room was, we kept that locker—

(*Upstage,* TOMBO *reenters with the* OPS OFFICER, *who begins to direct operations. Radio and phone activity continue under* HOGAN *and* SAMI.)

(*The board map lights up the checkpoints and roadblocks as they come into maximum alert action. Grid reference and center points are relayed to the helicopters, and the board indicates their direction of flight as they trace possible escape routes. Reports are scratched out, and later entered in the log. Small maps are drawn, then entered on the "master" map.*)

HOGAN: And *every*body loved her: When the principal came over the loudspeaker our senior year, he said "Seniors may not share lockers. All four hundred seniors will have individual lockers. Except...for Laurel and Hogie."

(SAMI *holds only one firey instant staring at* HOGAN...)

HOGAN: *(Jolly, introducing himself at the party)* I hear they call you Sami the Sorcerer.

(*...then* SAMI *returns suddenly to his customary languid repose, wiping* HOGAN *from his mind—*LAUREL *disappears—and settling deep into his chair. Pause*)

HOGAN: Did you hear the one about the rooster who mounted the stump?

(*No response.* HOGAN *lets the question hang, tantalizingly. Then, just when he finally opens his mouth to go on, an answer rises from the motionless* SAMI.)

SAMI: In my world...the louder he crows, the sooner he's chopped.

HOGAN: Ooo! So my crow's too loud? Awright, awright, But my mama had similar sentiments, and *she* got used to me. So here's the deal. I put whatever's on my mind slap down on the table, and you learn to give back, you hear? Cause I'll stick to your hide. You're my man. You hear what I'm talking? In six months I've got to be ready to run this place. How about that? Commander. Of Observer Group Lebanon. So. Just what the hell is a Military Observer?

(*Pause. No response from* SAMI)

HOGAN: Are you or are you not the Information Officer?

(*Pause.* SAMI *still not looking at* HOGAN, *appears not to hear.*)

HOGAN: As I understand it, we investigate, liaison, make contacts.... Aw, come on, pick up your whistle. It's gotta be clearer than spit off a grasshopper, you'll never get a rest from me till you do.

SAMI: (*Low, easily, without looking at him*) What's a Marine doing here?

HOGAN: (*Exuberant*) A Marine? You're asking me about a Marine? Well... you know what they say: You want to serve your country—join the army. But Marines are more. You sign on with the Marines, you're joining....

SAMI: (*Cutting him off*) A cult.

(*Silenced abruptly, and off guard,* HOGAN *draws back, smiling.*)

SAMI: (*Softly*) You haven't answered me.

HOGAN: (*Becoming the politician*) Well now, you tell me—why are any of us here? There is a peace to be kept. Of a sort, at least. And this United Nations mission offers me the opportunity to help the people of Lebanon to...

SAMI: B S.

HOGAN: Begging your pardon?

SAMI: (*Turning to him, with a slow smile*) You know the idiom?

HOGAN: B.S.? (*Laughs*) Course ah do. But I didn't know you-all used such...

SAMI: (*Icy*) You don't know fuck-all about Lebanon, Colonel Hogan. You're here for pay-back.

(*Pause.* HOGAN *stares at him.*)

HOGAN: Seems I misjudged the available vernacular. (*Pause*) Well, if I don't know fuck-all, you sho-nuff are the man I need to see, ain't you.

SAMI: *(Suddenly chuckling)* You Americans have to be loved, don't you. That'll kill you every time.

HOGAN: The Marines came to Lebanon as peacekeepers in '82; why shouldn't I sign on with the U N now?

SAMI: *(Sharp, a slap)* Because Lebanon spat out the Marines.

(HOGAN's *smile disappears.* LAUREL *comes racing to the locker.*)

SAMI: Wham-bam, bye-bye barracks? Unless...you're telling me Marine Corps honor includes "turning the cheek"?

(HOGAN *eyes* SAMI *stonily a moment, then recovers his bounce.*)

HOGAN: *(Buoyant)* It's a new world out here, eh Sami? Long time since Turkey was milking this place. You know, I heard one about a Sultan who tried to move his wives out of Beirut, so they lured him down to the grand bath house, and when he was steamed up and completely naked, they...

SAMI: *(Gently cutting in)* Marines are trained for one thing, Colonel Hogan. And it "ain't" peace.

HOGAN: No, no, now just a fucking minute, there. You're forgetting. All of you here, the fourteen nation's worth of men I'll have under me are all soldiers, Mister Sami. And because the U N asks these fighting men not to *fight*, there's another quality they require, a quality possessed by the United States Marine above any soldier on God's green earth, and that, Mister Sami, is discipline!

SAMI: *(Cool)* Like you showed in Beirut?

LAUREL: *(Throwing them a look)* Whooee... Right on!

HOGAN: *(Hot)* No Marine ever, *ever* fired without being fired upon!

(*The burn registers, then* HOGAN *catches himself, pulling out with a laugh.*)

HOGAN: Hey, hey! My cheeks getting red? You know what Laurel would say?

SAMI: You let yourselves be tricked.

HOGAN: *(Immediately back in Beirut)* We went there in good faith. And they threw roses. Roses! We went under strict rules— we could not fire. And by God we upheld them! *(Transitionless jump, erasing Beirut)* I tell you, if Laurel got a load of these cheeks she'd holler, way across the hall....

LAUREL: *(From across the hall)* You're either going through menopause, or having a heat flash, or what is it?

HOGAN: That's how crazy she was. I mean it was 1963 or some goddamned year. We were no more than seventeen, and she'd blurt out the craziest....

SAMI: You crept step by step into the war.

HOGAN: *(Lost, getting erratic)* American boys believed, *believed*, Mister Sami, that some good was being served. And at home they said no one was being shot at, the dying boys were only accidents!

SAMI: And then...the barracks blew up.

(Pushed to breaking, HOGAN is tripped into another time, as though he's forgotten something.)

HOGAN: Todd. Todd?

SAMI: *(Confused, watching HOGAN)* Who are you talking... Colonel?

(Then, catching hold of a past vision, HOGAN relives the explosion.)

HOGAN: Sunrise—it's...on Beirut, golden wash, gleaming, pastels... astonishing. And Sunday. The boys are nested, having a last dream, an extra half hour. *(Beat)* I saw the grin. Like he was sharing a secret. Dark beard, dark blue shirt, blurred past the gate. His big truck, yellow, sitting alone in the lobby, looked silly. Then came the orange white flash, too loud to hear, glued skin to my cheekbones; wind...lifted the rooms, pulled out their air, set four stories down in one pile.

Some boys woke with their ceiling in bed, and the floor above and its ceiling and the next, too strange to believe. They said God, oh God help me. Now I lay me down to sleep. The boys covered in ash, scattered, parts without arms, without heads, caught in trees, never woke, but were found by boys who never slept after. And the boys with head and arm hanging free, bodies crushed between slabs, dripping slow...red on grey ash, when they woke, those were the worst.

(HOGAN stands still, unable to speak. SAMI, close to him, speaks softly.)

SAMI: And I say payback. Payback is why you're here.

HOGAN: *(Haggard)* Todd. Where are you?

(LAUREL turns from the locker, suddenly draped in a large black shawl.)

HOGAN: *(Shouts in terror)* Todd!

(TOMBO shouts, jubilant, as the OPS OFFICER moves quickly out, exits. LAUREL is gone.)

TOMBO: They've got a witness!

(HOGAN turns his back, his light disappears. SAMI, reaching for him, buckles over, then lifts a hand to clutch TOMBO's shoulder, as TOMBO races on with his message.)

TOMBO: *(Breathlessly)* Somebody saw a brown Volvo pull out of a side road, flag down the oncoming U N vehicle, and drive off with the Colonel. *(Checks the map)* Must be the road from Al Qulaylah. That's all I got. No license number.

SAMI: *(Stony)* And no radio check. Was his Cherokee...still running?

TOMBO: Yes. And keys were still in it.

(SAMI *turns away, putting a hand to his forehead.* GABE *stands, horrified.*)

TOMBO: So we know what we're looking for.

(*Board lights are coming on to indicate the partial cordon now going into effect, and movement of battalion search parties east across UNIFIL Area of Operations, toward, but not into, the Tyre pocket.*)

SAMI: Until they switch vehicles.

VOICE-OVER: India 9 to Delta 1. Over.

TOMBO: That's the first chopper. It's up.

GABE: *(At the mike)* Delta...delta, I... Tombo, could you... (*He is turning away from the mike, nauseated.*)

TOMBO: What. *(Sees* GABE's *condition)* Gabe, lad, are you all right?

GABE: I...I was O K. But now we know...someone saw him taken, I...

(TOMBO *pushes* GABE's *head between his knees, and takes over the mike. The* OPS OFFICER *is returning, with some charts in hand.*)

TOMBO: Delta 1 here. Go ahead, India 9.

GABE: *(Head down)* Sir, I know Colonel Hogan. I was with him in the field, and... Sorry, sir. Sorry.

OPS OFFICER: Deep breaths, Corporal.

VOICE-OVER: We've got heavy mist in the Wadi Ain Baal. Visibility, one quarter kilometer.

(*The* OPS OFFICER *leans over* TOMBO *to answer. Phone is ringing;* GABE *leans up to answer.*)

OPS OFFICER: *(Into mike)* A Volvo won't go off-road into the Wadi. (*To* TOMBO) What's the elapsed time?

TOMBO: *(Checking clock against his log)* Twenty-two minutes, sir.

GABE: Force commander on the phone, sir.

OPS OFFICER: *(Nods, speaks into mike)* India 9, stay over the Tyre to Buryash road. *(To* GABE) I'll take it inside.

(OPS OFFICER *exits upstage.* GABE *sits, weakly.*)

GABE: *(Slightly wild)* We need a search team in the Wadi.

TOMBO: *(Puts a hand on* GABE's *shoulder)* The OPS Officer's got teams moving in from the battalions, look. *(Indicating the map)* Bloody hell. Tyre is where we need the cordon, and we can't touch it! That's where they'll go.

SAMI: Is anybody on the ground in Tyre?

TOMBO: Yes, the Observer Group Team, but...

SAMI: Get them. Have them stand by to liaise with Amal. *(He is walking to his own desk phone.)*

TOMBO: *(Warily)* Amal...? With Sharif's militia?

SAMI: Your cordon isn't closed! *(Into phone)* Khalini kalem ma'a Sharif!

GABE: We can't go in there, Sami.

SAMI: What good's a fence with a hole in it? Ttsaa! *(Into phone)* Hathe Sami, UNIFIL. Fee darori. [THa rori]

TOMBO: Don't you think Sharif *did* it? He could finger him from his headquarters.

SAMI: *(Slams down phone, reaching toward his keyboard)* Whoever did it, as Hogie would say, they've sho-nuff hog-tied us. And I...had better do the job I'm paid to do.

(SAMI types. The screen could flash the type large.)

SAMI: "MARCH 16 14:15 HOURS. COL WILLIAM HOGAN, LEADER OF THE UNITED NATIONS' OBSERVER GROUP LEBANON REPORTED MISSING. *(He hesitates, then corrects his error)* "REPORTED...ABDUCTED"

(Simultaneously, HOGAN comes striding towards him, now dressed fully U N— in his own Marine uniform with sky-blue cravat added, and sky-blue beret replacing his helmet. He stands apart with a grand "Arabic" gesture.)

HOGAN: Salaam, my friend!

SAMI: *(Goes on typing)* Go away! "...SEIZED BY THREE GUNMEN WHILE ENROUTE FROM TYRE."

HOGAN: Got it down, now. What do you think? How'm I doing? Got it down, man. You guys are all about *gab*. You just talk the enemy to death. Hell, I can do that.

SAMI: *(Hands to his own temples)* I don't hear you. You aren't here.

HOGAN: It's like I said to the Secretary of Defense, I said, Cap...

SAMI: The *enemy*, Colonel?

HOGAN: No enemy. No enemy. There *is* no enemy. Right?

(Pause. HOGAN grins at SAMI. SAMI sighs, laughs in spite of himself.)

HOGAN: But what should I call it when this Israeli, this I D F cadet shoves the barrel of his M-16 upside my cheekbone? Well, I grin a touch, and give the young man to understand that he's just waving his pink ass in the breeze, seeing as how the piece he's got cocked in my face was built, bought, and delivered by the U S of A and consequently has standing orders *not* to shoot a Marine.

SAMI: *(Staring at him)* Miraculous. Hogie, the peacekeeper.

GABE: *(At board with earphones, suddenly)* Checkpoint 1-23 has a brown Volvo approaching at speed. Looks like it's going to try to run the block!

(TOMBO jumps to the radio. SAMI has stood to listen to the checkpoint incident, but HOGAN, at his shoulder, stays with him, chattering affably.)

HOGAN: Told you I'd catch on. Nothing sissy about it. Matter of fact, takes more nerve than packing a piece! Whole passel a' fancy dancin'—hell, it's like playing chicken.

SAMI: *(Confused)* Chicken?

TOMBO: Those lads are balmy!

HOGAN: You get 'em talking, you just Columbo the living hell out of them. Just say any damn fool thing in the beginning. How's their girlfriend, do they know any hot places around....

TOMBO: They're standing in the path of the Volvo.

HOGAN: And you know, people like it, they really do.

GABE: The Volvo'll kill them.

TOMBO: Jesus, Mary, and Joseph, they're after standing across the center of the road!

(TOMBO and GABE draw a breath, waiting. SAMI is galvanized, pulled between the radio action and HOGAN.)

SAMI: *(Demands of HOGAN)* And if they're already shooting? Then what.

HOGAN: *(Leaping, now that he's gotten a response)* End run. We do an end run. That's the stuff.

TOMBO: It worked!

SAMI: End...run?

TOMBO: The Volvo stopped!

HOGAN: Team of two, you know. We go in twos.

SAMI: *(Pressured)* I know. I know!

TOMBO: They stopped it! They found him. B'gory, if this won't make a poet of me...!

(Long pause, everyone with held breath)

TOMBO: *(Disbelief)* It's clean. No Hogan. The Volvo's empty.

(TOMBO and GABE deflate, SAMI collapses into his chair, HOGAN cheerfully closes in on him.)

HOGAN: So we two split, circle round behind the guys, both sides. Then, while this guy's shooting, you tap him on the shoulder and say—uh, what are you doing? Well, right off, he's got to think. He's thrown off guard.

So first he thinks "what kind of asshole's gonna walk up, when I'm in the middle of shooting, and ask me what I'm doing? He can see what I'm doing!" Well, but in order to answer he has got to think what *is* he doing, and as he thinks, the instant he does, you're on him. You say, look, my partner's over there talking to the guy you're shooting at, and we think it'd be a great idea if you both would just stop—say, five minutes from now. Just a sec, let me check. *(Mimes talking to radio)* —How bout in five? Yeah. O K. Five it is. *(Snaps his fingers, grins at* SAMI*)* See it's hard to argue with that. First, 'cause it's the last thing you expect, you know, when you're screwed up to shoot. The other guy is supposed to screw up and nail you back. But then, after a while, you get conditioned: When the guy rolls up in the blue and white jeep, you're gonna hafta stop your shooting. So pretty soon you don't even bother to start. And that's what's called Pavlov's strategy.

(SAMI *laughs loud.* HOGAN *is gone, as lights flash bright, and* SAMI *realizes something has changed.* GABE *and* TOMBO *are rising, open-mouthed, to focus on a regal figure dressed in a Western suit and a white turban.)*

TOMBO: ...Sami? It's Sharif.

(GABE *and* TOMBO *stand at attention,* SAMI *also stands, taking in the image.)*

GABE: *(Hushed, to* TOMBO*)* Have we moved on his territory?

(TOMBO *shushes* GABE *with a gesture.)*

SAMI: *(Bows elegantly)* Wahsahlan.

SHARIF: *(With a nod)* Assalaamu aalaykum.

SAMI: *(Returning the greeting)* Waalaykuma issalaam.

SHARIF: And so you are bound to protect me. Does it disturb you?

SAMI: Why should Allah's law disturb me?

SHARIF: Of course. You put it well.

SAMI: *(Pause)* A delight, my dear friend, as always. You will take coffee?

SHARIF: Forgive me. Time does not allow... Your commanding officer?

(SAMI *nods to* TOMBO, *who exits toward the* OPS OFFICER's *office.)*

SAMI: *(Eyeing* SHARIF *carefully)* I expect the weather in Tyre is...

SHARIF: *(Returns the look)* Not too stormy.

SAMI: *(Unsatisfied, broaches:)* You got on well with Colonel Hogan?

VOICE-OVER: *(In background)* Oscar 3 to Delta 1. Over.

(GABE *looks at them and moves to radio anxiously.)*

GABE: Delta 1. Go ahead.

SHARIF: *(Smiles slightly)* Colonel Hogan. An American. Very...energetic.

VOICE-OVER: I've got two more witness reports.

GABE: Uh...hold, please.

SAMI: *(Smiling at* SHARIF, *wanting more)* You met for perhaps an hour, and now...

SHARIF: *(Cold anger)* Now...I am assaulted.

(TOMBO *reenters, stands at attention, indicating that* SHARIF *may see the* OPS OFFICER. SHARIF *nods, sweeps past him and out.)*

TOMBO: What was that about? Why, for the love of Mike, is Sharif here?!

GABE: Go ahead, Oscar 3. I can take them now.

SAMI: *(Sits heavily)* I don't know.

VOICE-OVER: A witness says there was a switch. Hogan is now in a white Peugeot.

GABE: Where did this switch happen?

TOMBO: Did Sharif come here to deal? Already?

SAMI: You think he's got Hogan.

TOMBO: Don't you?

(SAMI *looks at* TOMBO, *but doesn't answer, speaking instead to himself.)*

SAMI: *(Murmurs)* Like stealing a baby.

(HOGAN, *in shirt-sleeves and baseball cap, and* LAUREL—*both carrying books—are approaching the locker from different directions.* SAMI, *hearing them as nightmare confusion, puts a hand to his forehead. The sequences are tight, overlapping—)*

LAUREL: *(Calling)* Hogie! I've finally got you figured!

HOGAN: *(Reaching for books)* You ready for English? Got the poem?

LAUREL: How does a short tubby guy like you get all the "lookers"?

HOGAN: Bet you didn't memorize it.

LAUREL: Bottom line, Hogie: You have got...the "S" word. The big "S."

HOGAN: *(Suspicious)* What "S" word?

LAUREL: *(Reciting instead of answering)* "It was many and many a year ago..." Don't tell me, I'll get it.

> VOICE-OVER: Another witness says the Volvo skidded in mud, and crashed into a truckload of oranges.
>
> GABE: *(Into mike)* Location? Give us a location.

HOGAN: What "S" word?

TOMBO: *(Insistent, standing over SAMI)* Why wouldn't Sharif do it? He has Hogan in Tyre, he puts a finger out, and that's it. *(Snaps his fingers)*

LAUREL: Sensitivity!

(A loud buzzer sounds. HOGAN and LAUREL respond.)

LAUREL: What's that?

HOGAN: Assembly Alert. Come on!

(HOGAN slams locker door. He and LAUREL move away from it.)

LAUREL: Got it! "...there lived a maiden whom you may know."

TOMBO: You here, Sami?

HOGAN: Wrong. You left out "in a kingdom by the sea." *(Fast)* "It was many and many a year ago in a kingdom by the sea, that there lived a maiden..."

LAUREL: You think we'll miss English?

HOGAN: You better hope so. "...whom you may know by the name of Laurel Marie."

LAUREL: You nut, that's not her name!

HOGAN: So what? If it helps me remember? *(Shouting)* Those two free, Skipper?

TOMBO: Why couldn't it be Sharif?

SAMI: *(Dragging his mind back to TOMBO)* Wasn't it a poet you wanted to be?

TOMBO: I *could* do mysteries.

SAMI: If Sharif "put a finger out and that's it," then why is he so angry?

(TOMBO is stymied. HOGAN moves, as though shoving into a row of seats.)

HOGAN: "And this maiden she lived with no other thought..."

LAUREL: Whoever heard of a kingdom *not* by the sea?

AMPLIFIED VOICE: We have grave news from Cuba, a country just ninety miles off our coast....

HOGAN: "...with no other thought than to love and be loved by me." *(Sits)*

LAUREL: *(Sitting)* What's happening?

AMPLIFIED VOICE: Nuclear missiles capable of striking all points of the United States are enroute to Cuba on Soviet warships.

HOGAN: My God. This is something.

AMPLIFIED VOICE: President Kennedy is dispatching forty ships and twenty thousand men, including six thousand Marines... *(The voice continues under.)*

HOGAN: Laurel...if they don't back down and we don't back down...

LAUREL: Only ninety miles over the sea? Be serious.

HOGAN: ...it's war.

LAUREL: *(Pause, then, shocked and angry)* Forget it.

(LAUREL *turns, is gone.* TOMBO *has a hand on* SAMI's *shoulder, and will pour him a coffee.* SAMI, *unknown to* TOMBO, *is hearing* HOGAN. *A radio interrupts.*)

HOGAN: Sami, she was just...

> VOICE-OVER: Italair 2 to Delta 1. Over.
>
> GABE: Delta 1, your flight pattern cleared. Go ahead.

HOGAN: You know how, when somebody is so strong in you...

> VOICE-OVER: Visibility is poor. And my windshield wiper...

HOGAN: ...their personality is so...impressing....

> VOICE-OVER: ...she's banged out.

HOGAN: ...they kind of lift you, make you more than yourself?

> VOICE-OVER: In this rain, we have for sure only forty minutes of daylight remaining.

SAMI: *(On his feet, answering* HOGAN*)* Yes. Yes!

(SAMI's *phone blares. He snatches it.* HOGAN *is gone.*)

SAMI: UNIFIL. Sami here.

(SAMI *throws his hand up for attention, makes a signal.* GABE *reaches to amplify the caller's voice, and tape it.*)

SAMI: Who is this?

VOICE-OVER: Name not important. We have Colonel Hogan. If you wish him alive, you arrange us.

SAMI: Who are you.

VOICE-OVER: We...Islamic Revolutionary Brigades. That is all. *(The phone clicks, dead.)*

TOMBO: *(Looking at* SAMI*)* Islamic Revolutionary...?

SAMI: There's no such thing. *(Beat)* I never heard of them. They don't exist.

TOMBO: Go on, you know there's a gang born every minute.

SAMI: Run it. Run his voice again.

(GABE *runs the tape.* SHARIF *reenters unnoticed, stands listening.*)

TAPE: "Name not important. We have your Colonel Hogan. If you wish..."

SHARIF: It's a fake.

SAMI: *(Startled, eyes* SHARIF *sharply)* You think so, my friend?

(TOMBO *answers intercom buzz, nods, gathers several double sheets from the log.*)

SHARIF: Clearly a fake. Where is the snapshot? A picture of the Colonel?

SAMI: Perhaps...there hasn't been time for them to...

SHARIF: If they had proof they would offer it.

SAMI: No doubt you understand these affairs better than I.

SHARIF: No doubt. What have you so far? Give me your reports.

(TOMBO *stands ready to hand over the sheets he's collected, but looks to* SAMI, *hesitating.*)

SHARIF: Don't fear me, my friend Irish. It is Sheik Hajj who has done this crime. And beyond the crime, he dares assault my honor. Colonel Hogan was my *guest*.

(SAMI *looks at* TOMBO, *and* TOMBO *hands* SHARIF *the log sheets.*)

SHARIF: Now... (*Takes them*) Amal will find him!

(SHARIF *swiftly turns and exits. The others stand stunned, looking after him. But* SAMI *is focused on* HOGAN, *dim, behind the screen.*)

GABE: Was that an angel of deliverance? Or...

TOMBO: Or...?

GABE: Or...a you-know-what.

TOMBO: Now, now, Gabriel, no tribal messing, please.

GABE: But you don't know. They can pretend friendship, and then...

TOMBO: *Will* Amal help us, is the question. What can he do?

GABE: Who is this "Hajj"?

(TOMBO *looks at* SAMI, *who doesn't answer.*)

TOMBO: Hajj is Hizballah: Party of God.

GABE: (*Frightened, mouths*) "Hizballah?"

TOMBO: Hajj *and* Sharif. I say they're in it together.

GABE: I've got to go.

(*Static interrupts. Even* GABE, *panicking, about to run out, hesitates, watching the blinking that fills the main projection screen.* HOGAN *is visible behind it, in uniform, but as he speaks he's being faded out.*)

SAMI: Where are you, Hogie? Can you reach me?

HOGAN: (*Appears dazed*) I could have made a mistake. Could be I bit off more than I could chew.

SAMI: You Yankee bastard...

TOMBO: (*Wondering who* SAMI's *talking to*) Sami...?

SAMI: ...help us out here. Report!

(TOMBO *is directing* GABE *to make dial adjustments, trying to bring in a picture.*)

TOMBO: Somebody's sending. But I can't seem to get it....

HOGAN: *(Chuckling, punch-drunk)* But I tell you, Sami—women have definitely got a part missing: because...no matter how carefully you explain War to them, they don't get it. They just don't.

SAMI: Hogie...

HOGAN: And you don't even realize they're not with you, because they nod "yes yes" all the while you explain. But when push comes to shove, watch out. Cause they nev-er believe in it. Never.

SAMI: Hogie!

(*First the words "Transmission in progress" appear, then, slowly, an image comes into fuzzy focus in front of* HOGAN *himself. The image is an I D with* HOGAN's *picture on it. It is in Hebrew. Its number will become clear enough to read. As the three stand staring at it,* SAMI's *phone blares. He picks it up.*)

SAMI: UNIFIL. ...Ishar! Do you know what's going on down here? ... Oh. ... Yes, it's just come up.

(*Looking at screen, he signals* GABE *to hit the speaker-phone.*)

SAMI: *(To* GABE *and* TOMBO*)* It's Ishar, from the paper in Beirut. He's sending...

VOICE-OVER: ...these photocopies were delivered here. You will perhaps know if they are...genuine?

(SAMI *lets the receiver slide as he watches the likeness come into sharper focus. Pause. Then, he says quietly—*)

SAMI: There's your snapshot. Look up the numbers, Tombo. *(Into phone)* Yes, I'm afraid they could be.

(TOMBO *is copying the number, then goes for a file.*)

VOICE-OVER: There's a note. I've done a rough translation. Are you ready?

SAMI: *(Heaves a pained sigh)* Sure.

(*The I D changes to a second one in English.* TOMBO *copies its number.*)

VOICE-OVER: William Hogan, an agent of America's C I A, who is using the activities of the United Nations Observers as a cover for his dangerous role of espionage, is now in the grips of our heroic strugglers.

(HOGAN *appears, dimly juxtaposed with his I D image, slowly becomes more present.*)

SAMI: C I A. Of course.

GABE: *(Involuntary)* No! Not a spy. He's a warrior!

TOMBO: Gabe, sweetheart, be cool. They always call them spies, don't you know. It's protocol.

GABE: There's nothing funny! That's what I know.

SAMI: *(Into the phone)* All right. Do these "heroic strugglers" have a name?

VOICE-OVER: Ooh, do they.

SAMI: I'm ready.

VOICE-OVER: Organization of the Oppressed on Earth.

SAMI: Good God. Never heard of them either. The Oppressed, notwithstanding, have a bigger budget than the Islamic Revolutionary Brigades, who could afford only a phone call. These guys have coughed up for audio-visual aids!

(Exasperated pause. Everyone's looking at him, HOGAN *included.)*

SAMI: All right—"Oppressed on Earth." Takes in quite a few of us. *(Pause, blurts into phone)* What do *you* think?

VOICE-OVER: In percentages? Ninety per says...it's Hizballah.

*(*GABE *sucks in his breath, stands.* HOGAN *breaks downstage to* SAMI's *desk.)*

HOGAN: What is this "Hizballah!" How am I supposed to keep these goddamed camel jockeys straight?

SAMI: *(To* HOGAN*)* Leave me alone! *(He hangs up the phone, demanding—)* The numbers, Tombo?

TOMBO: *(With file)* They check. They're his. I Ds belonging to Colonel William Hogan.

(They all deflate, shot down by this proof that HOGAN *is a prisoner.)*

GABE: I'm going.

HOGAN: *(To* SAMI*)* Tell me!

SAMI: *(Sitting to type)* Tell you, my ass. *(Typing)* "SHADOWY PRO-IRANIAN GROUP CLAIMS IT HOLDS AMERICAN MARINE."

*(*TOMBO *and* GABE *go on separately. Two conversations overlap.)*

    GABE: I have to get out there, Tombo.

    TOMBO: What?

HOGAN: *(Closing in over* SAMI's *shoulder, taking another tack)* Tell you what, Sami. You need a good scrub-down here.

    GABE: I've got to get out with the searchers.

HOGAN: No decent cockroach would be caught live in these piles of shit.

SAMI: *(Typing)* Don't touch a thing.

    GABE: I was Hogan's driver. I know where he's been!

TOMBO: What does that have to do with where he's going? I need you here.

GABE: I've got to go, Tombo.

TOMBO: Christ! Tell him, Sami.

SAMI: You're under orders, Gabriel. Stay put!

(Frustrated, GABE jerks and paces like a tethered horse.)

HOGAN: Isn't it these "Hizballah" who veil their women?

SAMI: *(As he types)* Lovely idea.

HOGAN: It's idiotic!

SAMI: Ah, your western poverty of imagination...

HOGAN: *(Circling up to look at the map)* Imagination, hell. This veil crap is pure paranoia.

TOMBO: *(At radio)* Now, here, listen, what's going on?

(He turns up a speaker and we hear a rousing harangue in Arabic, followed by prolonged cheering that continues under TOMBO and SAMI.)

TOMBO: Give it to us, Sami, what's he saying?

SAMI: It's Sharif...addressing his militia. It's...strict orders to find Hogan no matter what, leave no stone unturned, and not to sleep until they do.

TOMBO: Hey, hey!

GABE: Will they know where to look! Where to find these... "Oppressed"?

HOGAN: O K, show me here. Where do these Hizballah hang out?

SAMI: *(Typing)* Why do you want to know Hizballah? That's only one faction.

HOGAN: All right, all right, so give me the ball of wax.

(HOGAN steps up to the board so he can locate the factions geographically. At the same time, lights on the board will show SHARIF's Amal militia fanning out from Tyre to fill in a complete cordon around the Tyre pocket. GABE and TOMBO are oblivious to HOGAN and SAMI.)

HOGAN: I figure it's both Muslims and Christians I have to worry about—several flavors of each. *(As he names them, he points out on the map where each faction is concentrated.)* Besides that there are the Israelis, who don't belong here at all, the Palestinians, who are displaced, not to mention the Druze, who drop out of the mountains.

TOMBO: They're heading out. There goes Amal!

(TOMBO and GABE excitedly watching the lights fill the cordon, suddenly cheer.)

GABE: They're closing in on Tyre! *(Runs to radio)*

SAMI: Never mind all that. Focus on Muslims.

HOGAN: Partial to Muslims, are you?

GABE: *(At mike)* Delta 1 to Oscar 3. Over.

SAMI: In our AO the Christians aren't themselves anyway.

HOGAN: What's that supposed to mean?

SAMI: They're all Israeli-hired. They're paid gun-hands, some willing, some forced.

HOGAN: Forced?

VOICE-OVER: Oscar 3. Ready to copy. Over.

SAMI: *(Shrugs)* If you don't hire on, they slap your mother in prison.

GABE: *(At mike)* Contact O G L, Team Tyre. Amal is coming, joining the search! Over.

HOGAN: Come on, get to the Hizballah!

SAMI: Allah have mercy! The Muslims in our A O are mostly Shi'ites.

HOGAN: *(As though winding up a race, triumphant)* There we are! And the Shi'ites are mostly Amal or Hizballah! Right? Have I got it? *(Then, confused again)* But they're against each other.

(TOMBO *jumps up to relate what he's hearing to what he sees happening on the map.*)

TOMBO: My God...they're not stopping with car checks. They're moving on strongholds, searching houses, rounding up Hizballah!

SAMI: They're *all* against each other. Or not. Depends on the weather. You've got to understand *family.* Ra'ih al bagir ahsan min siyasat al-bashar.

TOMBO: See, they're deep now, going village to village, combing fields.

HOGAN: Which means what?

TOMBO: That's the woods along the Litani.

SAMI: Roughly: the intellect of a cow is better than the politics of the people.

HOGAN: *(Puzzled pause, then—)* By damn, I knew if I traced them back far enough they'd come out Americans.

(*They laugh loud,* HOGAN *throws an arm around* SAMI, *and they laugh more.* GABE *and* TOMBO *are engaged the whole time with radios—incident reports coming in from UNIFIL and Amal troops, relaying and logging them.*)

HOGAN: It's still paranoid bullshit, veiling their faces.

SAMI: Ah, no, it's wonderful! You haven't been properly introduced....

HOGAN: These men are scared shitless some other man's going to....

SAMI: No no no no, it's got nothing to do with the men. It's the *women*, man.

HOGAN: What?

SAMI: Imagine—beneath those fluttering eyes... *(Hushed)* ...they are utterly insatiable!

HOGAN: That's a fantasy the size of my....

SAMI: But so effective. You have no idea.

HOGAN: Yes?

SAMI: Yes...because by now... *(Mock whisper)* the women believe it.

(SAMI and HOGAN roar with laughter.)

> GABE: If Hogan's I D cards are already in Beirut, then he must be....
>
> TOMBO: An I D can cross a checkpoint without its person, you know. Damn sight more easily than *with*.

HOGAN: And you're telling me they keep it all in the family, right?

SAMI: Come here, my friend. Let me explain...

(SAMI drawing HOGAN to sit by his desk; intimately—)

SAMI: This you need: It's all family. Family and hard life. Picture the desert. Someone takes your water—that's it. No second chance. So you take no chance. Someone hurts you? Two eyes for an eye. Payback, but harder—it's a rule. Now, as to whose eye it is? You never know. Friends may turn. Enemies may turn. You watch out for the friends, and never kiss off the enemies. But it's family you trust: Me and my brother against my cousin. But, me, my brother *and* my cousin against you.

> GABE: *(At mike)* They think they've got three of the abductors—two from the first car. And three who'd been tailing him for a week!

SAMI: O K. Then there's God.

> GABE: And *another* with orders on him to take Hogan to Beirut!

SAMI: You believe in God?

> TOMBO: You see? They didn't get him through to Beirut.

SAMI: Is yours the true God? *(Beat)* There can only be one truth, and if it's true, *it* has the power. So why bother. All this fuss. Tsaaa!

> VOICE-OVER: Oscar 3 to Delta 1. Urgent. Over.
>
> GABE: Delta 1. Go ahead. Over.
>
> VOICE-OVER: Informant here, usually reliable, says Hogan's being held in the village of Brika at the home of Abdul Karim Hajj.

TOMBO: Hajj! Christ.

(The board lights begin to move, almost in a stream, east, across the entire map from Tyre toward Brika. TOMBO *and* GABE *stand awed.* SAMI *snaps to at the news of* HAJJ, *and stands, but still speaks to* HOGAN.)

SAMI: I'm Muslim. You know my prophets? There's Abraham...Moses...Jesus, yes, Jesus. So what? Same neighborhood. You think these stones don't know a little something? It's all one.

(The lights are moving in to circle an eastern village.)

TOMBO: Mother of God. It's Hajj's village.

(Entering on a whirl—a robed, turbaned, bearded HAJJ. *He stands blazing-eyed, imperious, at a distance. All, including* SAMI, *turn to look.* HOGAN *is gone.)*

HAJJ: *(Low, intense)* Call off your dog!

SAMI: *(Stunned, polite)* Sheik Hajj.

HAJJ: Madness. You loose it in my land. Innocents terrorized. One hundred fifty, I count them, dragged from their homes like lambs torn from the hillside!

SAMI: *(Moving slowly center)* Honored Sheik Hajj...

HAJJ: *(Interrupting)* Across three hundred square miles, on roads, in wadis, you rampage—and now, *fire*. Grenades heaved on rockets shatter the night. Is this your *peace*?!

SAMI: My humble apologies...but I'm sure the U N has not fired.

(Before SAMI *can appease the wrathful figure, a challenge cuts from the opposite side of the stage. It is* SHARIF.)

SHARIF: Come. To my face— tell me you don't have him.

HAJJ: *(Straightens, incensed, and spits out—)* Devil!

SHARIF: Does the snake deny the bird still whole in his gullet?

HAJJ: You dare the fury of God, Sharif. At this moment in Tyre forty-five scholars convene, appalled at your wantonness. You bleed your own body, Amal and Hizballah, both flesh of the dispossessed Shi'ite.

SHARIF: No one is bleeding yet. Except you, chewing your groin to loose your small toe.

HAJJ: Release my people!

SHARIF: Release Colonel Hogan.

HAJJ: Aha! The U N takes hostages now?

SHARIF: Only you do that.

HAJJ: Sharif, Sharif...do not tear this precious fabric. You're arresting innocents by the truckload!

SHARIF: I'll stop when you release Colonel Hogan.

HAJJ: You mistake my position. I know nothing.

SHARIF: I don't mistake your alarm. Am I hindering your plan?

HAJJ: The Jihad, the holy war, cannot be hindered.

SHARIF: Your "Jihad" is an obscenity smeared on the pure face of Islam.

HAJJ: This Lebanon, this beauty—endlessly trampled and raped...by the West, by the East, by Israel—she's ours. Help us, Sharif. We struggle, with nothing—women with rocks, children with shouts, old men with sticks—making miracles.

SHARIF: Islam condemns violence! You're abusing the faith!

HAJJ: Your heart, my brother, knows our pain. Is this our country? If it's my car and our road, why must I carry their license to travel it? Why may they shoot me if my car lacks a passenger? If I park my car to go gather berries, why may they blast it to hell?

When may I stop asking why? When they come to crush my village with tanks? When to stroll round my house in a tender moon is to die, because I'll be shot if I'm seen? When they round up our men, shepherds, tailors, and ship them away... Why?

Because they suspect, because we won't give in, because one has a name like one they've been given. When all these fail, and our leaders are still not destroyed, why do they plant death in our house of worship, thirty pounds, set to blast the moment relief, the meeting, the people...convene.

SHARIF: *(Silence, moved)* Yes, I know...who has done all this. *(Looks steadily at* HAJJ*)* How many *millions* of holy warriors...and weapons...do you need to rid the earth of Israel?

HAJJ: *(Cold fury)* Do not mock me.

SHARIF: You're a mad dog biting your savior.

HAJJ: The U N?!

SHARIF: They are here to move Israel *out*.

HAJJ: In what century?

SHARIF: Of course, you hate them. Does the U N need your love? Do you think they have Israel's? Hah! *Every*one hates them. That's how you can tell they're worthy of trust!

HAJJ: *(Pause)* You risk so much. Your officers are not with you in this.

SHARIF: So I dismiss them.

HAJJ: *(Shock)* You...dismiss them?

SHARIF: *(Aware of the danger)* Dirani and Kanso...I've done it.

HAJJ: *(Quiet)* Allah protect you.

SHARIF: In your village, the U N made flow the water, cleared death from the field, sucked clean your raw wounds. If you banish these blue berets, if you drive them away—deep in the night, your women will curse you.

HAJJ: You're blind! They breed spies. This Hogan, this C I A spawn, burrows deep. If they shield him, they too are betrayed.

SHARIF: So you violate a guest.

HAJJ: I am not involved.

SHARIF: It was a terrible mistake.

HAJJ: One tainted American? What is he worth?

SHARIF: To Americans, something.

HAJJ: Americans, hah! They're faithless.

SHARIF: If their faith has grown weak...

HAJJ: They have lost their soul. And they disrespect ours—as though the faith of eight hundred millions counts as nothing in the eyes of God. They will learn.

SHARIF: But your "innocents" have confessed the abduction.

HAJJ: Torture creates eloquent lies.

SHARIF: These orders to transport Hogan were forged?

HAJJ: *(Reads from paper* SHARIF *extends)* They don't name me.

SHARIF: Of course not. But my eye sees you. There is more than one prophet in Islam: two days before this abduction, it was planned in your home. The chief captor returned there straight after the crime. Here is a list of all who participated. And remember, Hogan called you from *my* home.

HAJJ: I know nothing.

SHARIF: And nothing of the "Organization of the Oppressed on Earth"?

HAJJ: Look a million years. It doesn't exist.

SAMI: *(From a distance)* It made the evening news.

HAJJ: Unless it wishes to exist. That's the beauty of Hizballah. No cards are held, no lists kept, you feel this "resistance of the poor", but you could never draw our picture—except as a breathing organ, with each cell sensing what concerns his fellow.

SAMI: *(Moving casually forward)* Did you catch it? The evening news.

HAJJ: *(Flashing)* Of course.

(SAMI *goes about pouring cups of dark coffee.*)

SAMI: Your predecessor would be proud. Old Harb.

(HAJJ's *eyes flash, then soften at the mention of Harb. He moves in to* SAMI.)

HAJJ: You knew Harb? Not so old. A saint, a prophet, cut down early. Me in his shoes is blasphemy. *(Pause)* But yes, he would. He would have seen the news, and been proud. We would have watched together. He was poorer even than I. And it killed him.

Because he had to take the evening news at his neighbor's T V. And because they knew—knew he had to see, to know, to learn—he was an easy shot. Israelis could crouch in the shadow, at the corner of his house as he shuffled, exhausted, home to bed. So they splattered him over his step. And his place fell to me, too young, too unworthy. I can only honor him.

SAMI: Every anniversary...you honor him. By attacking Israel. He died, let's see, in '84? So in '85, a communique promising revenge; in '86, ambush of an Israeli convoy; in '87, two bomb attacks; and in '88, now, on the anniversary, March 16...

GABE: *(Starts involuntarily)* No...

SAMI: The abduction of Colonel Hogan is your commemorative act!

(HAJJ *smiles appreciatively.* GABE, *breathless, confused, makes his way out as fast as he can.*)

TOMBO: Gabe!

HAJJ: Clever, Mr Sami. But I didn't set the date. He did.

(HAJJ *turns abruptly, is gone in a whirl. The lights drop simultaneously, to shadows, except for* SAMI's *desk.* SHARIF *walks briskly out, and* TOMBO *is gone.* SAMI *sits at his desk, staring forward, dazed.*)

SAMI: *He* did? He set the date? Hogie, what have you done?

(Static of audio transmission beginning. The video image forming out of the dark is a tape of HOGAN *as hostage. He speaks—)*

TAPE: I, William Hogan, in order to get me released...

SAMI: Hogie... Hogie!

(SAMI's *shout materializes* HOGAN *himself, out of uniform, carefully cleaning out the locker.* LAUREL *comes, bouncing across a distance with a bold chant.*)

LAUREL: Hell, no! We won't go! Hell, no! We won't go!

(The hostage tape continues under LAUREL's *chant. When she reaches the locker she starts cleaning her stuff out of it, and chattering breathlessly—)*

LAUREL: Get the lead out, Hogie. I got the last posters hung. Moved the rally up to noon, right after graduation. That way we'll snag a thousand more off that crowd. Hey-hey, "Dump the Draft" is big news! You finish writing in my yearbook?

HOGAN: *(Handing her the album)* Yeah, but don't.

LAUREL: Don't what?

HOGAN: Don't look at it now.

LAUREL: What do you mean? *(Opening it)* Of course I get to...where is it?

HOGAN: Not back there. It's with the pictures.

LAUREL: *(Finding his writing)* Oh, wow—a whole bunch. "I was a child and she was a child..."? *(Looks at him)* Oooo, poetry! "...in this kingdom by the sea, but we loved with a love that was more than love, I and my Laurel Marie..." *(Pause, reads silently, then stops)* Hogie, what is this?

HOGAN: What.

LAUREL: What are you saying here? *(Pause)* Why did you let me go all this time, and not even...!

HOGAN: Why?

LAUREL: I've always just...been relaxed with you. I just felt safe.

HOGAN: I never let anything hurt you.

LAUREL: Hogie...

HOGAN: I never *will* let anything hurt you.

LAUREL: ...you know I'm marrying Todd.

HOGAN: So. What does it matter?

LAUREL: What does what matter?

HOGAN: What does it matter *when* I tell you?

LAUREL: Hogie!

HOGAN: Everybody's full of surprises. *(Taking uniform coat from locker)*

LAUREL: What's that?

(HOGAN *putting on Marine jacket and hat*)

HOGAN: How do I look?

LAUREL: *(Upset)* What?

HOGAN: You like it?

LAUREL: No! Are you crazy?!

HOGAN: See...you can't understand everything.

(HOGAN *is walking away, a small package in his hand. She shouts after him.*)

LAUREL: Hogie! You're not a killer! Hogie? Do the Marines know you get seasick?!

(SAMI *sits dazed.* HOGAN *moves straight toward him, exchanging his hat for the U N beret.*)

SAMI: *(Murmuring to himself)* I should have been here, I should have...

HOGAN: *(Moving to* SAMI, *beaming)* How do I look?

SAMI: *(Out of his daze)* What?

HOGAN: *(Handing* SAMI *the package)* Bottoms up! This whole operation asks your permission to rev up, shut down, or take a piss. Come on, live a little!

SAMI: *(Not knowing which scene* HOGAN's *in)* What's...?

HOGAN: For Sami, on my graduation!

(SAMI *realizes he's holding a package, fumbles it open. It is a crisp new blue beret. He is moved to tears, but covers gruffly.)*

SAMI: I can't wear this. I'm a civilian.

HOGAN: As new leader of Observer Group Lebanon, I say—if you can't wear it, nobody can.

(Shaking his head, SAMI *puts the beret on top of the highest pile on his desk.)*

HOGAN: Who do you think you're kidding. It's *you*. Put it on!

(SAMI *whips around, grabbing* HOGAN *by the arms, trying to make this memory talk to him in the present.)*

SAMI: Hogie...Hogie, I need you to talk to me *now*.

(But HOGAN *doesn't hear him, is pulling* SAMI *out of his chair, and will move him.)*

HOGAN: I'm gonna let you in on something classified, Sami. Double-malt, coming up!

(The radio is crackling. A transmission begins.)

SAMI: *(Insistent)* Hogie, I need your help. Tell me what you've done!

HOGAN: This is something big.

VOICE-OVER: A late bulletin reveals that Colonel William Hogan is present in Lebanon on secret assignment from the Department of Defense.

(SAMI *tries to twist around to pay attention to the radio, but* HOGAN *has him firmly by the arm, and is moving out.)*

HOGAN: This is top secret...the most powerful piece of information I've got. And when I tell you, you'll know how much I trust you. Because this is foolproof. Absolutely. Get you in anywhere. No matter how formidable the opposition. No matter how pathetic your showing is. Are you ready? *(Pause)* Tell her she's looking beautiful.

(They are gone. The image of HOGAN *as hostage remains as house lights come up. A saxophone plays* Stranger on the Shore.*)*

END OF ACT ONE

ACT TWO

(On screen, Beirut, all else dark. Prom Music: Stranger on the Shore, *segues into machine gun and small-arms fire—then music swells over again, as isolated light comes up on* HOGAN, *juxtaposed against the screen image. Like his hostage video, he wears a heavy sweater.)*

HOGAN: The woman on the bridge, that's it. *(Pause)* Funny. Me here. Sort of like, against all odds, you know what I mean, one of those things that just has to be? Like the woman on the bridge. *(Pause)* There was this bridge, the deadliest crossing in Beirut—buildings towering, both sides, called sniper's alley. And for days there was murderous fire. Nothing live dared sniff the air. Any vehicle forced to cross would hit the bridge at racing speed.

Then, in the midst of all the firing, for no reason, a woman began to cross, on foot. The instinct was—scream, stop her, pull her back. But she couldn't hear, she was too far, and she kept crossing. Then it happened. *(Awed)* Silence. The firing stopped. Why? Maybe they were all just...astonished. The report said "A woman, showing signs of insanity..." That was how they made sense of it.

And that's me: the woman on the bridge.

Well, what am I supposed to do?! Say "insanity," shrug it all off? Then what can I tell Todd— "These people make no sense. We don't know what we're doing here. I was afraid?"

(Pause, then HOGAN *looks suddenly upstage, and, in another light, we see* LAUREL *moving slowly in his direction, draped in the black shawl, and carrying a baby.* HOGAN *quickly stands, facing her. She speaks to him from a distance.)*

LAUREL: Good of you to come.

(Pause. Both are uneasy.)

LAUREL: I tried to stop Todd going, too, you know. So he just...proved me right. Got shot clean out of the sky.

HOGAN: The choppers are dead-on targets. I...I'm sorry.

LAUREL: Yeah. *(Pause)* Are you out then?

HOGAN: Uh, no.

LAUREL: Then where's your uniform?

HOGAN: I, uh, didn't want to upset you.

LAUREL: Oh. Thanks.

HOGAN: And I give you this: it's a useless war.

LAUREL: *(Vague)* What?

HOGAN: Nam. Totally useless. I'm sorry.

LAUREL: Yeah.

HOGAN: He's so beautiful.

LAUREL: Beautiful?

HOGAN: Todd Junior.

LAUREL: *(Looks at baby; her face finally softens; she begins to exit.)* Boy, I hate to think of the stories you could tell him.

HOGAN: *(Following her)* Guess I could.

(They look at each other and laugh. Then, as they walk away—)

LAUREL: Remember the time we got hauled into McKnight's office, and he...

(Lights coming up on same set as in ACT ONE. TOMBO is at the board, looking at the map, speaking into the mike. A Radio Beirut broadcast is in progress.)

TOMBO: *(Into the mike)* O K, got you located. Over.

VOICE-OVER: The latest information on Colonel William Hogan reveals that he holds top security clearance in the United States and is present in Lebanon....

(SAMI comes hurrying on, stops dead, hearing the broadcast.)

VOICE-OVER: ...on secret assignment from the United States Department of Defense.

TOMBO: Jesus, Mary and Joseph. What do you think?

SAMI: *(Continuing straight to his desk)* Did you lay out Hogan's file?

TOMBO: It's all on your desk. But what do you make of that?

SAMI: *(Reaching for a newspaper)* Bullshit.

TOMBO: But Hajj fingered him. He said Hogan set the date. Now...which brilliant lad was it said Hajj would be trouble?

SAMI: That was just double-talk, a fat load of Shi'ite Taqiya.

TOMBO: A load of what?

SAMI: Taqiya—justified deception, very religious. Roughly translated— you can lie all you want whenever you're cornered and outnumbered. Where's Gabe?

TOMBO: With a search party. Probably Sharif's militia.

(Search parties, now scattered through the whole of South Lebanon, are highlighted on the board.)

SAMI: What?!

TOMBO: He just ran.

SAMI: That's a court martial!

TOMBO: *(Shrugs)* He's Fijian.

SAMI: What does that mean?

TOMBO: Miraculous sweet people, but monstrous fierce when they've decided on something.

SAMI: *(Reaches for the beret on his desk, remembers* HOGAN *giving it to him)* He's just...frightened for Hogie.

TOMBO: Well...if these "holy martyrs" think Hogie's a spy, they won't leave much of him to worry over, will they?

(SAMI *and* TOMBO *hold, looking at each other.)*

TOMBO: Thinking you might put it on, are you?

(SAMI *flings down the beret, and whips open a newspaper to glare into.)*

SAMI: No labels for me.

TOMBO: *(Watching him)* All alone in the glen. *(Beat)* Did the Undersecretary General get down all right?

SAMI: Sixteen minutes late. *(Finding an item)* Here: says Hogan was "assigned in Washington". Doesn't mean a thing. Pure bull.

TOMBO: He'd probably fancy being called a spy. *(Mimics* HOGAN Well, when I advised the Secretary of Defense, I said to him. "Cap— here's how you..."

(The teletype clatters on, delivers a bulletin.)

TOMBO: *(Getting up to read it)* Whoop...

SAMI: *(Annoyed)* So he drops names. So? *(Sighs)* It's harmless.

TOMBO: This'll be the update.

SAMI: No one with top security clearance gets sent here from the States. Too dangerous. Make too inviting a target.

TOMBO: Listen here, the Pentagon's making a counter-claim: "Colonel William Hogan was employed as a Junior Administrative Assistant, together with fifty-two others, to Casper Weinberger."

SAMI: *(Stunned, groans)* Jesus Christ!

TOMBO: So he's got security clearance. Oooo, covering their tail with fluff. At forty-something they're calling him Junior?!

SAMI: Jesus Christ, why in bloody hell... Why *announce* it! When Americans, who vow virginal honesty, are up to some sniggling lie, they always blurt it out...*after* their pants are down.

(Upstage, RAYMOND, Undersecretary General of the United Nations stands looking at SAMI. He is well dressed in a dark suit and carries a briefcase. TOMBO, seeing RAYMOND, tries to cover SAMI's outburst.)

TOMBO: *(Embarrassed)* Mr Secretary, uh...Mr Raymond, would you like...

RAYMOND: *(Ignoring him)* Sami. It's vital that I know what I'm negotiating. If there's the least question about Hogan, end of story. It'll take a hundred years to rebuild our credibility.

SAMI: I know.

RAYMOND: So. *Is* he a spy?

SAMI: Makes no sense. No. The United States knows the rules.

RAYMOND: Yes, they know the rules. But they'd hock the Statue of Liberty to get a spy on the ground here.

SAMI: What do you mean? They have Israel. They can hire Lebanese. Why send a flag-waver like Hogan?

RAYMOND: Hizballah's rejoicing, I can tell you. They think they've got a prize songbird. How am I supposed to talk them out of it? Sami, I need to know. Why did *this* man get this assignment?

SAMI: *(Heaves a sigh)* Because he wanted it.

RAYMOND: Why suddenly a Marine? The Army wouldn't give up the position without a squawk.

SAMI: They didn't.

RAYMOND: Oh?

SAMI: There was a squawk. But Hogan pushed. And when he wants something, Allah help you. *(Fumbling in HOGAN's file)* And there was a string.

RAYMOND: What?

SAMI: *(Sighing, hands him a paper)* His recommendation was pushed through by...

RAYMOND: *(Reading)* Casper Weinberger. God! Then he *was* hand planted. *(Looks at SAMI)* Why are you dragging on this. Don't you see the position we're in?

SAMI: I just...don't think he's a spy.

RAYMOND: Sami, there's a reason he's here. The man is a neon target. The U S is naive, but this is just too stupid. The C I A's on me like a harpy. They want him out *now*. You have got to give me anything you know that compromises him.

SAMI: *(Bursting)* Everything compromises him. He just won't stop! Yes, he has an agenda. I'm sure of it. And not the U N's. But I don't think it's a C I A agenda either. I just....

RAYMOND: Don't think. Hizballah won't. And Sheik Hajj?! What's his connection? You know he's a number-one Israeli target. Another quick shake, and we'll mix up World War Three.

SAMI: Hajj will lay low.

RAYMOND: *(Sardonic)* You have his word, do you? *(Beat)* What about personals?

SAMI: A daughter. Wife, a professional. Clean.

RAYMOND: No weaknesses? Apart from an incorrigible mouth. No other women?

SAMI: No drunkenness, no drugs, no sleaze, one fantasy.

RAYMOND: What?

SAMI: Laurel Marie. Particularly inspiring young lady. Long ago.

RAYMOND: My God. Is there anyone whose brains this cowboy hasn't boiled to sugar!? Answer me this: Given his record—had his companion car turned around, and *not* been able to find Hogan's vehicle, in other words, lost him, in a restricted zone, knowing he was alone, against all regulations, wouldn't you have let it go, assumed he was "doing his thing," never even have reported it, let alone—as an abduction?!

(SAMI *glares at* RAYMOND, *not answering.* RAYMOND *moves to exit.*)

SAMI: Hogieee! Who in hell do you think you are?! Keep your nose where it belongs!

(HOGAN *is lit, at a distance.*)

HOGAN: I make you uncomfortable? I don't quite fit? Maybe that's cause I've got faith. Sort of like Hizballah. Hah. They'll have to respect that, won't they.

SAMI: *(Rattling tirade)* You go into restricted areas without notification or clearance. With no one in your car, and no companion car. Alone! You set up meetings without registering. You meet with people you have no authorization to, in places you have no authorization to be. You never do radio checks!!

HOGAN: And you...have plainly never heard of the lone wolf.

SAMI: A lone wolf is a desperate animal.

HOGAN: Aw, shucks, you're just on my case because....

SAMI: And you above *all*!

HOGAN: ...I'm a Marine.

SAMI: *And* because you're American. Don't you even read the papers?! Americans are not allowed to travel to...

HOGAN: I am proud to be an American.

SAMI: A little less pride, and you might *be* one longer. None of you can be trusted! Since Viet Nam, you've got one big societal screw loose. You can't so much as settle on how to sit down.

HOGAN: I will go wherever I think I need to.

SAMI: Not while you're wearing the beret! This takes dedicated balls. You think we won it easily? The right to walk between?

(He strides to the board map of UNIFIL, pounds on it. TOMBO *is not aware.)*

SAMI: This agreement is made of fairy dust! It floats lightly in the fractured minds out here only as long as they believe that we are neutral. And honorable. Absolute credibility. That's our power. The only one we've got. But it's enough. See how immense? A whole people is cradled here in its fragile net. But, the least fray...and it snaps. Do you want to be the guy responsible for....

HOGAN: No! But *this* Marine is not going to get blown into chunks without knowing why!

(SAMI stands openmouthed; TOMBO *interrupts, while* HOGAN *stomps away and disappears.)*

TOMBO: Sami... *(Uncertain how to deal with him)* Sami, there's this woman....

SAMI: What?

TOMBO: This woman keeps calling you. Says Hogan gave her the number.

SAMI: He's slipping, Tombo. He's becoming...thin...in my head.

(On the map, the lights are now moving erratically, in disorder.)

TOMBO: The Hizballah say he's already in Beirut....

SAMI: Soon he'll drift away.

TOMBO: ...but Reuters says he's been smuggled west into the Bekaa Valley.

SAMI: Bullshit. We've got to find him before...

TOMBO: But have they slipped him through our net?

SAMI: He's being walked out across the Litani.

TOMBO: What?

SAMI: Not over the bridges we're sitting at so nicely like they knew we would.

TOMBO: Walked?

SAMI: Yes, walked. Your generation does partake upon occasion? Walked. I'm sure of it. *God*, I need a connection. I'm losing hold of him.

TOMBO: They found nothing at Brika? At Hajj's?

SAMI: No. At Hajj's...it was quiet. What will they do to him, Sergeant Bohanna?

TOMBO: *(Doesn't want to answer)* I took this woman's number. If you want to call. *(He extends a note toward SAMI.)*

SAMI: What do I want with some woman! *(Beat)* It's not his wife?

TOMBO: No, she's... They're briefing his wife at the Pentagon.

SAMI: Tombo, our friend is either a clumsy spy, or an extraordinary innocent.

TOMBO: If he's a spy, he knows what they'll do to him.

(SAMI looks sharply at TOMBO, who backs off with a joke.)

TOMBO: And to think me mum's happy as a daisy down the glen to be packing me off on me third tour to the Lebanon. To her mind, as pious butchery goes, I'm safer here than in Ireland.

SAMI: *(Not deflected)* And if he's an innocent? At least he's a brave one.

(TOMBO looks at SAMI uneasily.)

SAMI: *(Snapping)* Pull Hogan's schedule from the meeting day. Where was he before that? Who was with him? Who did he talk to?

(SAMI is concentrated on the idea of HOGAN, and at a distance HOGAN appears, trying to speak to SAMI in the present, but times and places become confused.)

HOGAN: Sami...I'm a little uneasy. I'd like to run this mess by you.

SAMI: Fine. Where are you?

HOGAN: Can you read me?

(But LAUREL has appeared, distracting HOGAN.)

> LAUREL: Already, you're a Major, Hogie? Don't tell me.

SAMI: Hogie!

> HOGAN: Hey, did you see? Todd Junior's as high as my chest!
>
> LAUREL: Check again. He was standing on his toes.
>
> *(They laugh warmly together, but LAUREL is fading.)*
>
> HOGAN: You know, you are the...

SAMI: Talk to me straight!

HOGAN: How could I say to her "You're me. I mean, my whole spirit."

SAMI: Who has you, Hogie!

HOGAN: "You made me who I am."

SAMI: *(Shouts, erasing HOGAN)* Tombo! What will they do to this "spy"?

HOGAN: *(Fading)* Sami...? Things aren't working out like I...

TOMBO: Here's his sched...

(Seeing SAMI's face, TOMBO is unable to avoid answering any longer. On the screen, quick flashes of hostage torture photos)

TOMBO: Disorientation.

HOGAN: *(His last call)* Sami...? *(He's gone.)*

TOMBO: Sensory deprivation. They'll try to make him lose hope.

SAMI: *(Tight)* Hah. That'll take a while.

TOMBO: Then they'll start the questioning.

SAMI: "Questioning." Yes. It doesn't take much "questioning" before the only good hope is that you'll die soon. Of course, not Hogie. He's a Marine!

TOMBO: *(Worried for him)* Sami, it's no use to...

SAMI: *(Exploding)* And who cares about *him*? Tell me. Nobody wants to take the damage, do they? What is this man —expendable, worth less than the *face* anybody's losing? The U S face trembles because they've bungled again, the U N's face, because what if he's a spy? Everybody's scurrying to cover. It's Amal who's doing most to find him. Arabs are risking more than any of us! And what for? Because if Hogan is successfully taken, they lose *face*.

(The phone blares. TOMBO jumps to answer it.)

SAMI: Where are those witness reports!

TOMBO: *(Answering)* UNIFIL.

SAMI: *(Finding the reports, reads emphatically)* "Hogan was driving a U N jeep station wagon from Tyre to..."

TOMBO: *(To SAMI)* It's the woman again.

SAMI: What woman?

(Onscreen, a photo of RAYMOND. His voice-over, being interviewed—)

RAYMOND: *(V O)* We do not recruit spies, nor do we hire them.

TOMBO: Her name's Laurel.

SAMI: *(Stunned)* What?

(SAMI takes the phone. As the RAYMOND tape goes on, LAUREL's voice, amplified, overlaps, and then overpowers RAYMOND's.)

RAYMOND: *(V O)* Here is an American who came to Lebanon...

LAUREL: Sami...you *are* Sami? Hogie said you were the man to know. I mean, really connected.

RAYMOND: *(V O)* ...to take part in an enterprise set up to assist...

LAUREL: He said everybody in the friggledy world is calling you. So I thought....

RAYMOND: *(V O)* ...the withdrawal of Israeli troops from Lebanon...

LAUREL: Sami, we are getting the most god-awful news back here. And I wanted you to know...

(A closeup photo of LAUREL *is projected, large, as her conversation continues, vividly amplified. Focus on* SAMI, *transfixed)*

LAUREL: ...that whatever happens, Hogie'll land on his feet.

RAYMOND: *(V O)* ...to support Lebanese sovereignty and Lebanese state institutions.

LAUREL: Cause before he came out to you-all, he called and said "Laurel, save my seat at the twenty-fifth reunion, cause this Lebanon is my last tour, then I'm out for good, so I'll see you in July." Now, Sami, you're familiar with how god-awful stubborn he is, so you *know* he will make it.

SAMI: *(Shaken)* Laurel...?

LAUREL: And besides, you mustn't be feeling bad, because I know that whatever damn fool mess he's in, he damn sure asked for it. You couldn't stop him. Any more than you could shut his mouth. We're just alike in that. You know when the two of us get going, both at the same time, you can't make out a single word? It gets so bad I finally yell— "would you suck in a breath, it's my turn!"

SAMI: Laurel, I'm...glad to hear from you.

LAUREL: Just try to find him, Sami. I know he's a pain. But he's not finished. He always bounces.

*(*SAMI, *helplessly moved, looks to* TOMBO, *who's handing him several reports. The phone slides out of* SAMI's *hand,* LAUREL *rattles on,* HOGAN *appears, easy, released, as though he's floating, out of time.)*

LAUREL: You know why? Cause in spite of all his brass he does have that big "S" word. You know it, Sami. Did he tell you his story about the mosque?

HOGAN: I was wandering in this town, and just headed for the stand-out spot—a cathedral. Except it wasn't—or it was—because the whole insides, the giant grey stone, and pillars, and arches had been made white—just opened, lifted from inside by this wash of white over everything.

(While HOGAN *goes on with intimate delicacy, hushed awe,* SAMI *tries to squeeze an answer from reports in his hand. Their speeches overlap easily, with* HOGAN's *continuous, and* SAMI's *dropped in.)*

SAMI: *(Reading)* "He was driving a U N jeep station wagon from Tyre to Naquora...

HOGAN: And everything else was gone. No altars, no founts, benches, chairs. So it was...immense. White.

SAMI: "...behind a similar vehicle in which two other Observers were travelling.

HOGAN: But with carpets, colored carpets over the whole expanse, lapped over and over each other.

SAMI: "The first vehicle went around a bend in the road....

HOGAN: Low dias-platforms, low railings with whorled posts...

SAMI: "...and when they noticed Hogan's car wasn't following....

HOGAN: ...stairs to a turret gaily painted, astonishing green, red, yellow.

SAMI: "...they stopped, drove back, and found the station wagon abandoned."

HOGAN: It was rape. Muslims had raped this Cathedral.

(SAMI *looks up at* TOMBO.)

HOGAN: But it was so light...

SAMI: Hogan made a phone call.

HOGAN: ...restful—like wandering into someone else's heaven.

SAMI: There was a meeting—for what?

HOGAN: Only delight, peace...

SAMI: Niceties, feeling out politics, and what...special agenda?

HOGAN: Outside, was a circular fountain, with spigots all round the bottom.

SAMI: *(Remembering)* Hogan made a phone call! Sharif said so.

HOGAN: Like Jesus, I guess, you wash your feet before entering.

SAMI: Find out to where.

HOGAN: So I did.

TOMBO: How can I? He's lucky if he....

SAMI: *(Exploding)* Try!

HOGAN: You know, Laurel always laughed at my feet.

(SAMI *finally looks at* HOGAN, *is caught off-balance between times.*)

HOGAN: *(Chuckles)* She'd be at the edge of the pool and I'd come down after practice and try to fool her, hands over her eyes, but she'd let out a husky giggle—

LAUREL: "I see Hogie's feet! Nobody else has toes that look like fingers. I swear Hogie, they do, exactly like fingers!"

(SAMI *sees* LAUREL, *and is drawn into the fun.*)

HOGAN: Well, I'd say, don't you worry. It's one of my superior advantages. You know the girls are always looking out for what my *hands* are up to, when what they ought to do is watch out for my toes!

(LAUREL, HOGAN, *and* SAMI *laugh buoyantly, as* LAUREL's *image fades.*)

HOGAN: *(Pause, then from quiet)* Remember your first love?

(SAMI *sighs, and settles back.*)

SAMI: "It was many and many a year ago...."

HOGAN: "...in a kingdom by the sea." Do you know that piece?

SAMI: She was leaning over the fountain. The only place she was allowed to come alone.

HOGAN: To draw water?

SAMI: *(Nods, smiles)* Water's a potent God among Turks.

HOGAN: Bet she had fire beneath the veil.

SAMI: She didn't wear a veil.

HOGAN: "I was a child and she was a child...."

SAMI: And I lost her so soon.

HOGAN: But it was like we stood apart from everything, stood together, looking on. *(Chuckles)* I'd be making out in the back seat, and watching her go to it in the front. And smack dab in the middle of a heavy kiss, Laurel would open her eyes, see me looking at her, and we'd both crack—burst out laughing.

SAMI: Wait, wait. Why was she in front?

HOGAN: Imagine how pissed our dates would get?

SAMI: Then, you weren't together?

HOGAN: Laurel and me? She was never mine.

(RAYMOND *is standing behind them. Dim. Pause*)

RAYMOND: He's dead.

(SAMI *scrambles to his feet, stands staring at* RAYMOND. HOGAN *disappears.*)

RAYMOND: That's the report. Of course there are three versions. One says "died during torture," another "while trying to escape," another....

SAMI: Where's the body?

RAYMOND: Body?

SAMI: Do you have it? If you don't have the body, he's not dead. It didn't happen.

RAYMOND: *(Pause, looking at him)* Perhaps.

SAMI: Besides, he has a date next July.

RAYMOND: A what?

SAMI: I need time to...to go over every step from the beginning. There may be something obvious we're overlooking, some contact he made, some....

RAYMOND: Sami, I'm in touch with all the heads of factions.

SAMI: There must be something we can....

RAYMOND: You're very tired, Sami.

SAMI: You're right. He bent all the rules. I should have stopped him.

RAYMOND: How?

(SAMI *stands looking at* RAYMOND, *who holds a beat, then turns to go.* SAMI *shouts at the empty spot where* HOGAN *is in his imagination.*)

SAMI: You dumb Yank, is this the hero you have to be—dead?!

(RAYMOND *hesitates, looking back at* SAMI, *then exits as* HOGAN *breezes in, brightly attired in blue beret, cravat. Seeing him,* SAMI *doubles over in pain.*)

HOGAN: *(Grinning)* What about these hostages, Sami?

SAMI: *(Dull, dead)* What about them.

HOGAN: Well, do you think they're in Iran?

SAMI: I doubt it.

HOGAN: The Russkys had a method, you know, when three of their guys were taken, they identified the group that had taken them, ambushed a member of it, and...no rhetoric, no bargaining, just sent his body back to his fellows—minus the testicles. Sort of a gesture.

SAMI: I heard.

HOGAN: Now, that's called talking the language! Not exactly our way. But the important thing is, you've got to stand there without blinking, get in the swing, don't you know?

(HOGAN *stands thinking, no response from* SAMI, *as though he's frozen— unwilling to enter the scene and unable to prevent it from happening.*)

HOGAN: Then where do you think they're being held? Beirut?

SAMI: Perhaps.

HOGAN: They say a lot wind up in the Bekaa Valley. But who's got them?

SAMI: Usually you don't know.

HOGAN: Usually radical Muslims. Usually tied to Iran, like the Hizballah. *(Pause)* You know, the way I figure it, we may not see eye to eye, but what those guys have got in spades, and what they are bound, therefore, to admire, is conviction, bravery, determination. The thing would be... to approach them boldly, and never, no matter what, never show fear. They'd have to admire that. Honor is everything to them.

(Satisfied with his summation, HOGAN *winds up.)*

HOGAN: So Iran calls the shots?

SAMI: *(Can hold out no longer)* Hogie...

HOGAN: They're sold, aren't they? It's all a matter of money.

SAMI: What do hostages have to do with anything?

HOGAN: Why won't you tell me about it?

SAMI: I don't know. It's not my business. And it's not yours.

HOGAN: I thought you were the Information Officer.

SAMI: We're not an intelligence service. Get that straight!

HOGAN: I know, I know. Learn something by chance, it's fair, but if you're "ever-caught-gathering" aieeeeee.

SAMI: We *have* no enemies. So there's nobody to spy on. Got it?!

HOGAN: Aww, tell it to the Israelis.

SAMI: *(Suddenly hot)* Shut up about Israelis! You think they've got no complaints?! Every bullet from every side kills *some*one's child.

HOGAN: You're clamming up on me.

SAMI: Did you hear the one about the South Yemeni cabinet meeting?

HOGAN: What?

SAMI: Ali Nasir had heard of some disagreement with his policies. So at the meeting his attendants latched the door...and machine-gunned the cabinet. Who had weapons of their own. Like a sealed chamber explosion, the walls became quite...messy.

HOGAN: What has that to do...

SAMI: I want you to be aware what comes of a little suspicion. And not one of the families held the slightest grudge. *(Lifting a paper from* HOGAN's *file)* What asinine joke is this?

HOGAN: What you got there, my C V?

SAMI: This multi-paged, single-spaced listing of every assignment you ever had, every brass tea party you ever sat in on?

HOGAN: It's my bio, biography. Just an...introduction.

SAMI: And you've been handing these out everywhere. So your contacts will know who they're dealing with?

HOGAN: Sort of. I guess you'd say...

SAMI: And it doesn't occur to you that your little "calling card"—with its "National Security Council" this, and its "C I A" and its "Secretary of Defense" that— is like batting a red flag at so many wounded bulls?!

HOGAN: Look Sami, it's a small matter of diplomatic courtesy.

SAMI: Courtesy, my balls! It's bald and idiotic self-promotion. You have got all the position you can get, Colonel. You're not bucking for Defense Director of Lebanon.

HOGAN: *(Laughing)* I pity the guy that is.

SAMI: Not funny! Listen to me: macho is not cool. They will skin you alive and wear your skin to the palace.

HOGAN: Sami. There are some folks who come out here to float, and there are some who intend to improve the situation.

SAMI: *(Wearily)* Oh yes?

HOGAN: Yes. And, whether you believe it or not, one man can make a difference. That's why we're going to take a drive tomorrow out to Irishbatt's A O.

SAMI: *(Checking incident reports)* Irishbatt? What's happening? Nothing in the last forty-eight...

HOGAN: I want to meet the folks at Khirbet Silm....

(SAMI stops dead and holds.)

HOGAN: ...and you're my number-one escort-translator. You can keep me out of trouble, make sure my overtures are delivered in a correct light. Hell, I won't even know what twist you put on them. See how I trust you?

SAMI: *(Controlled)* You want to go to Khirbet Silm.

HOGAN: Sure do. And you know what the Force Commander's tune is: *(Melody,* Teddy Bear's Picnic*)* "If you go out in the woods today you better not go alone."

SAMI: *(Laughs)* Khirbet Silm?

HOGAN: What's funny?

SAMI: It will not happen.

HOGAN: What do you mean? Reno Team call there all the time.

SAMI: Reno Team are not dangerous. You want to go because I told you the Hizballah headquarter there.

HOGAN: Well, you did.

(Silence. SAMI *will not reply.)*

HOGAN: *(Clears his throat)* M Os, apart from their "military observing", *make contacts* with Mukhtars, Sheiks, Lebanese Army....

SAMI: But why Hizballah?! They're not causing us trouble.

HOGAN: Well, Sami, you know....

SAMI: *(Biting him off)* I know you've been quizzing every local on the road—"Where are the Hizballah?" "How many are there?" It shoots back through the mouths of boys. "Tell the Yankee to mind his own business." With a big nose and a bigger mouth, you've marked yourself—"enemy." So there is no chance, in this life or the next, that I will take you to Khirbet Silm!

HOGAN: Why, Mr Information Officer, are you losing faith? Do you find me suspicious?

SAMI: *(Beat. Then, sharply)* I find you insane. So who cares if you're suspicious.

HOGAN: Insane. Because I vigorously pursue my mission?

SAMI: "Your" mission? The only mission here is that of the United Nations. *Nations*, not States. Can you grasp that you are *not* the most sacred thing in the world, and maybe not even the most important.

HOGAN: Maybe you're just stuck. Maybe you're carrying some kind of Turk guilt that makes you impotent. Because your granddaddy was ambassador when, after milking and kicking them for years, they starved the Lebanese in their own fertile country to feed the Turkish army.

(SAMI *straightens, glaring at him.*)

HOGAN: You just sit here and stew. Maybe you like the power, sitting in the center of this hell hole, knowing the score. Maybe if something actually got accomplished, you'd lose your spot!

SAMI: *(Pause)* You intend to improve things?

HOGAN: How could I make them worse? This place is a preview for the apocalypse.

SAMI: Blood also comes with birth. *(Pause)* Let me tell you straight: We do not advertise. I am not a P R Office. I am not your goddamn agent. I've got no idea what position you're auditioning for, and I don't want to know, but if it has anything to do with American hostages you are betraying me, the U N, *and* the U S. You stand to destroy the U N mission, not to mention America's place in it, and to cause your country still more grief. If you are not such a traitor...

HOGAN: What happened to your fearless "walking between the fire"?

SAMI: Where do you think you are—play school?! Did you ever not get your way? You're still in a goddamned horse opera. We have heroes, yes, but not glory. This *is* the valley of the shadow, and we have to bring *everybody* through. It's more than you, than me, than anything you can dream. And before it's about triumph, it has to be about *surrender*.

(*Beat. The projection screen erupts with the whirl of an ambush capture—helicopters, guns, night fire, screams.* SAMI *whips around to look at the screen, then back again to* HOGAN, *but* HOGAN *is gone, and, instead, calls to* SAMI *from another location.)*

HOGAN: Sami? Sami, it's getting rough out here, and I don't have....

SAMI: What? What's going on?!

(TOMBO *has leapt to his feet.* RAYMOND *is running in. The teletype rattles.* SAMI *lunges for the sheet, pulls and reads it.)*

SAMI: Oh...my God.

(Upon reading the sheet SAMI *still holds,* RAYMOND *exits swiftly.* TOMBO *is looking at them.)*

SAMI: *(Handing* TOMBO *the sheet)* Hajj. It's Sheik Hajj.

TOMBO: What?

SAMI: He's been ambushed, kidnapped, stolen right out of his home.

TOMBO: By whom? Sharif?!

(SHARIF *becomes visible, standing upstage.)*

SHARIF: *(Furious)* Why?!

(SAMI *and* TOMBO *turn to him.)*

SHARIF: Why have you done this!

SAMI: Sharif, if this is a trick...

SHARIF: Why take *him*? What did you hope to gain!

SAMI: You're not making sense.

SHARIF: The Israelis attacked. You must have agreed. How else could they move?

(Media/radio eruption—reports begin coming in. Printing on screen. Voices overlap, mesh. TOMBO *is pulled to the teletype, receives a printout.)*

VOICE-OVER: Israeli Commandos abducted Sheik Abdul Karim Hajj, a leader of Hizballah, from his home in southern Lebanon early this morning....

SAMI: You know better.

VOICE-OVER: ...The twelve commandos, arriving on helicopters and carrying pistols equipped with silencers, fatally shot a neighbor in the head when he looked out his door as the group left....

SHARIF: Do you know how it happens? In the middle of the night. Just when you settle, feeling safe for day. When the knock comes your sons are startled awake, grabbed, bound, taken. Their father is bound, taken. Their mother, their sisters, bound.

Then a neighbor, alarmed at the scuffle, opens his door to offer something...anything, just wide enough to call, just wide enough for a bullet to answer. The good neighbor sprawls on his threshold, with nothing to offer, forevermore. *(Pause)* All this happened...to the holy man I delivered you—terror in his soft family night. And you tell me I'm not betrayed?

I am mocked! I risked my people and my name, turning them in bloody hand against each other in support of what? —of an American, who feeds Israel, who murders us in our beds. This is devil's work, and you, with your false peace, are the devil's own machine. I behaved as a man of honor. Hah. Honor!

SAMI: Sharif, we are as shocked as you. This was a criminal act.

SHARIF: And what will you do about it? Will your precious Americans, who mother Israel, scold their spoiled child and make him give back the priest he stole, the neighbor he murdered? Of course not. The spoiled child will sit glaring from his corner, his bloody prize squashed behind his back.

The West supports West, because we have no soul. We are bloody Arabs. To us, you are people of the book, the Bible/the Koran, Jews, Christians and Muslims. We know the book is one, delivered alike to all humans. But you know it not. To you, we should not exist.

SAMI: You forget me. *I* am Muslim.

SHARIF: You are nothing! A man who splits his soul between East and West, what can be left of you? Where to call home?

SAMI: The world is wider than your East and West.

SHARIF: Yes, and you'll drift upon it, perpetually in search.

SAMI: Home is wherever your heart does its business. Mine is here, where nothing is ever clear, where betrayal rips the belly of understanding. Me, against the scream. Forever searching a place—to lay a mother, a child, an old man to rest. It's the only home I have. And the only honor. A curse on all your religions!

(SHARIF *nods without speaking, turns to exit.*)

SAMI: Sharif. You've done much. I know what it's cost you. Please...

SHARIF: I cannot hear you. This act of Israel's flings all Arabs in one lump against the wall.

SAMI: Help me save my own.

(SHARIF *stops as if struck.*)

SHARIF: Your own? Is it that? Or is he the enemy.

SAMI: I...don't know.

SHARIF: Is Hogan your family?

SAMI: He's no different from you and me. Just...searching for home.

SHARIF: So. You put life above honor. A Yankee life.

(SAMI *is speechless. They face each other.*)

SHARIF: I mourn for you. You've drunk the Yankee poison, their almighty power. Oh, he smiles on you, but he made you his fool. He'd click his tongue at a thousand of your family on fire, then order his lunch.

SAMI: *(Hoarse)* Sharif...

SHARIF: You will learn. The Yankee smile lies.

(SHARIF *is leaving, but* TOMBO *springs forward impulsively.*)

TOMBO: Excusing me, your...honor, but...

SHARIF: You're addressing me?

TOMBO: Your militia did search magnificently, and did apprehend a number of suspects, and...

SHARIF: And. *(Glances back at* SAMI, *then at the packet he's carrying)* ...I do have the grace to pity you.

(SHARIF *hands the packet to* TOMBO *and leaves.* TOMBO *starts to hand the packet to* SAMI, *but* SAMI *is still staring after* SHARIF, *so* TOMBO *tears it open while reports of the kidnapping come in via radio, television, and screen, overlapping, simultaneous.*)

VOICE-OVER: Israel's kidnapping of a fundamentalist Shi'ite Muslim cleric...

VOICE-OVER: ...predicts that Muslims across the entire world will retaliate for Hajj's abduction.

SAMI: *(Numb)* What's there?

TOMBO: *(Flipping frantically through paper)* Interviews...with the witnesses they arrested. He left us what he learned. Look!

(TOMBO *hands the opened packet to* SAMI, *and twists to read the teletype, which rattles as audio reports continue.*)

VOICE-OVER: Amal and Hizballah, long rivals, joined hands today to fight Israel, ordering a general strike that paralyzed large parts of Lebanon.

(TOMBO, *reading the teletype printout, looks at* SAMI, *hesitant.*)

SAMI: *(Throws up hands)* Tsaaa! What can we do with this...trail of remains?

TOMBO: Sami...this may not be official, but...it's come through the teletype and...I think you'll have to broadcast it.

(TOMBO *hands* SAMI *the printout. He reads it.*)

SAMI: No, Allah, please... *(Looks at* TOMBO*)*

SAMI: Did you notify the OPS Officer?

TOMBO: Yes. He's speaking to New York and Washington.

SAMI: *(Numb)* Of course.

TOMBO: There is one thing about it.

SAMI: *(As he turns dully to his keyboard)* What?

TOMBO: Maybe this means he's not dead.

(SAMI *begins typing.*)

SAMI: *(Hoarse)* "THE ORGANIZATION OF THE OPPRESSED ON EARTH SAID TODAY IT WOULD EXECUTE MARINE LIEUTENANT COLONEL WILLIAM HOGAN UNLESS SHEIK HAJJ, KIDNAPPED BY ISRAELI TROOPS, WAS RELEASED."

(*Then* SAMI *stands frozen, hearing a broadcast.*)

VOICE-OVER: The following statement was delivered, typewritten, to Radio Beirut a few minutes ago: "We will execute the American spy by hanging at exactly three in the afternoon".

SAMI: *(Bellows)* Get Raymond back!

TOMBO: Sami. Sami! You'll have to talk to the press. *Washington Post* is on the phone. *New York Times* and the A P are backing up the wire.

(RAYMOND *comes slowly to stand opposite* SAMI. SAMI *faces him, across the stage, motionless, phone in hand.*)

RAYMOND: It's confirmed. The execution is set for three P M. Unless Sheik Hajj is released.

SAMI: What can you do?

RAYMOND: *(Pause)* Fadlallah will meet me.

SAMI: Fadlallah! What about Hajj?

RAYMOND: That's up to Israel.

SAMI: Will they release him?

RAYMOND: The United States will press them.

SAMI: *(Repeating)* Will the Israelis release Hajj?

(RAYMOND *simply looks at him an instant longer, then turns and leaves.* SAMI *throws up his arms, shouts.*)

SAMI: I want those witness reports!

(*There is a media burst.*)

VOICE-OVER: The White House views the threat to kill Hogan gravely....

VOICE-OVER: Outrageous, uncivilized...

VOICE-OVER: Syria, Saudi Arabia, the Soviet Union have been asked to "use whatever influence they have to put a halt to any killings."

SAMI: *(Still shouting)* Where are you now, you smart-ass bastard!

(*Shots of hostage captivity, tapes sent of hostages, home shots, accompanied by brassy big band sound of* Stranger on the Shore. SAMI *raises the phone to his ear.*)

SAMI: *(Abrupt, flustered)* Yes. All right: we have had no, repeat, no information on whether Colonel Hogan is still alive. Therefore we are not, repeat, not in a position to assess the latest threat.

(Pause. SAMI *listens at the receiver, while watching images of* HOGAN *in captivity, which flash on the screen.)*

SAMI: I have nothing to say. No comment. *(Beat, listening)* Yes, the United Nations Undersecretary General, Mr Raymond, is meeting at this moment with Sheik Mohammed Hussein Fadlallah...spiritual leader of Hizballah, hoping to arrange a stay of execution. Yes, execution. The Hizballah maintain Hogan is not their hostage, but is standing trial as a spy.

*(*SAMI *listens impatiently, then blurts, too fast, in order to sign off—)*

SAMI: Yes. A spy. We just hope he is well and alive and will be released immediately.

*(*SAMI *hangs up fast, looks sheepishly at* TOMBO.*)*

SAMI: He's slipping away. He's slipping. *(Then barks to cover his fear)* Get Sharif back!

TOMBO: *(Bewildered at the request)* I don't think we can.

*(*GABE *stumbles in, dirty and exhausted.)*

SAMI: I want to talk to him. I want to know what went on at that meeting!

TOMBO: I'll try.

SAMI: Give me Sharif's reports!

*(*TOMBO, *making the radio call, picks* SHARIF's *packet from where* SAMI *dropped it and hands it back to him.* SAMI *files through reports, as* GABE *moves forward, staggering.)*

GABE: Is there any more news?

SAMI: Where have you been?!

GABE: Out with the search, since...

SAMI: You look like hell.

GABE: There's only half an hour! I knew Colonel Hogan, and I....

SAMI: Know him. You *know* him.

GABE: I took him a message that....

SAMI: Think you can help him in this shape? Get sleep.

GABE: Thank you, yes, I'll....

*(*GABE *starts to leave, then, next to the screen, slides into a collapsed pile, too exhausted to move.)*

TOMBO: Sharif's gone to Beirut. Special meetings.

SAMI: I'll bet. *(Reading report)* "...three men carrying Kalashnikov assault rifles intercepted Hogan's vehicle..." *(Looks up startled, interrupting himself)* Sharif said it to Hajj! About the phone call Hogan made. Do you remember? As though they both knew something.

TOMBO: They were in it together. I said so then.

SAMI: Their fight was a fake?

TOMBO: Maybe. Or one betrayed the other.

SAMI: No...Sharif risked too much. He's practical, not a fighter. But he risked everything, all the Shi'ites! He was really trying to... "three men... intercepted Hogan's vehicle, shoved him into the trunk of their car, then sped off along a dirt road..." No, wait. Someone said he walked. Why would he walk. Did he? From his vehicle to theirs?

TOMBO: No one sees the same thing. We got three different car makes.

SAMI: *(Flipping through reports)* Where is it?

GABE: *(Shaking his head sadly)* He's a friendly guy. He always...

SAMI: *(Finding the entry)* This one. Says it's a woman, was digging vegetables, noticed U N Cherokee—because of its being white and the insignia, looked up again at the slam, then the Volvo skidded away.

TOMBO: That's all? She didn't see rifles?

SAMI: Why remark seeing rifles? Seeing them is definitely unremarkable. Even hearing them up the street only requires ducking, not remarking. Here it is: *(Reading)* "He *walked*, smiling..." Smiling?

TOMBO: *(Handing* SAMI *other papers)* Arrests records. Don't help much. They got two lads from the Volvo. One from the third car— Mercedes. But no hand knew what the other was doing. Never said Hajj was stupid, did I?

SAMI: You're sure Hajj planned it?

TOMBO: Sharif was. Here, even the would-be Beirut driver...his instructions only told him his part. If we tortured him we couldn't get more.

SAMI: Please don't...say torture.

TOMBO: *(Shrugs)* No good anyway. What can we do?

*(*SAMI *glares at him.)*

TOMBO: 14:45. Fifteen minutes till...

SAMI: *(Interrupts)* Leave me alone!

TOMBO: *(Looking closely at* SAMI*)* Has Hogan, ah...? Seemed like you were... in a way, ah, in touch with him?

SAMI: No. *(Looks at* TOMBO, *snaps)* That's finished.

(On the screen, photo image of a dignified woman. Her voice-over—)

VOICE-OVER: The news from Lebanon is not pleasant. I must, however, wait for confirmation. I've reached no conclusion.

GABE: *(Hushed)* Is that his wife? That's his wife, isn't it.

VOICE-OVER: The one thing I've learned is that the truth is hard to find. And I am determined to know the truth.

(As statement ends, RAYMOND *is standing upstage in long shadows. They all stand to attention, even* GABE.*)*

RAYMOND: Don't trouble yourselves. It was only smoke. And on the wrong road.

(Pause. Since they all hold, as though unable to breathe, he continues:)

RAYMOND: Sheik Fadlallah of the Hizballah is very opposed. Opposed to taking hostages. Opposed to killing innocents. Opposed, yes, but not, alas "master of decisions." *(Bitterly)* And so he *wasted* it. The priceless...time.

SAMI: *(Pause)* So you got nothing?

RAYMOND: What about Hajj. Have the Israelis budged?

SAMI: *(Looks to others, knowing the answer, then says)* Nothing.

(RAYMOND *moves swiftly upstage and off.* TOMBO, *earphones on, works the board, moving switches, answering lights.)*

TOMBO: *(As he works)* Call from the Soviet Union. There's one, France. India, Eygpt... Getting close. Syria. Iran!

SAMI: *(Pause)* How long do we have?

TOMBO: It's 14:55. Five minutes.

SAMI: God.

(HOGAN *appears far off, tied, extremely beat up, breathless, but laughing.)*

HOGAN: You'd hafta cheer, Sami... I'm holding out like thunder.

GABE: When I saw him, first time, he was scrambling up to the top of a redoubt, showing a young soldier how to stay covered on the way up. Him, a Colonel. After, he said "he'll follow me anywhere now."

HOGAN: Hey Sami, there's this little hitch....

GABE: He always said "you gotta be out there, gotta be with your men."

HOGAN: They just don't...believe me.

(Pained, SAMI *draws a breath lunging away from* GABE *as* HOGAN *fades, then stops dead at the reappearance of* RAYMOND.*)*

SAMI: *(To* RAYMOND*)* The Israelis. Will they...?

(All look at RAYMOND, *but he just walks downstage and sits, staring ahead.)*

GABE: *(Pause, while everyone is still)* We searched everywhere. Every inch, even of Khirbet Silm. Everywhere.

TOMBO: *(Low)* 14:59.

(Silence)

RAYMOND: *(Out of stillness)* I have to find...peers, you understand—diplomatically speaking. If you can talk, there's hope. It's a matter of finding the right person to talk to. To identify, then empathize, talk it through, it's really social, social...insinuation, among peers. *(Pause. Dead stillness)* But if you can't find them, or if they don't exist...

TOMBO: Fifteen hundred.

(SAMI slams something. Then silence again. Then lights on the board start, gradually, to recede and disappear. They sit, numb.)

GABE: What will hap...? How will we know?

TOMBO: An announcement. They always make a show.

GABE: How...long will it take?

(TOMBO looks at SAMI, shakes his head. RAYMOND leaves. Music: Stranger on the Shore. Projections of searches and of HOGAN, at different ages. SAMI holds as long as he can, then blurts—)

SAMI: Blowhard jackass! That's all he was.

GABE: *(Looking up, shocked)* Jackass...? Warrior. Real warrior.

SAMI: *(Flings a dismissive gesture)* Ffffft!

GABE: Don't say this, don't! He leads!

SAMI: Yes, where?!

GABE: Where?

SAMI: You're the jackass' tail.

GABE: Hogan knows me.

SAMI: What did he ever do for you?

GABE: Calls Fijians "best," the best! On my island, fruit grows warmly, but pride of tribe still rules. And Hogan sees me angry. Wanting to strike.

SAMI: So he calls you "son." Of a war-thirsty Marine.

GABE: No! He barks at me: *(Mimicking HOGAN)* "Don't you know peacekeepers are the only soldiers in the whole fucking world being trained for anything real! All you shoot-em-up guys are like so many billion dollar bombers — you're only built for a parade."

SAMI: *(Shaking his head)* The pied piper. With you trailing after.

GABE: He shows me how. Then says "Now who can challenge the peace of a Fiji warrior."

SAMI: *(Realizing)* You know what he was up to. Don't you!

GABE: *(Confused)* What was he up to?

TOMBO: *(Realizing)* You told me Gabe, baby. You knew where he'd been.

GABE: That's why they took me. Amal did. Along on their searches. Because I'd know him if...in case we found him. Because I'd been with him in Khirbet Silm.

SAMI: *(Startled onto his feet)* He *did* go to Khirbet Silm! *(Stunned)* While I was on leave.

GABE: I was always scared when we went out. I never doubted him, but....

SAMI: Never doubted what! What did he do there?! He betrayed all of us. Didn't he!

GABE: Sami...he's your friend!

SAMI: Friend? A two-faced Yank?! He risked your life, Gabriel! *(Grabbing GABE)* What did he do in Khirbet Silm!

GABE: Talked. Talked. Just said he wanted a meeting. Friendly. When I got the message, I never thought....

SAMI: What message.

(GABE *looks at* SAMI, *unable to answer.*)

SAMI: *(Panicked, shouts at GABE)* What message!

GABE: They sent it back with me. His contact in Khirbet Silm did.

SAMI: What message.

GABE: That...the date would be fine.

SAMI: The date. The date? *March 16!?*

(GABE *nods numbly, "yes".*)

SAMI: He did it himself! He set up a meeting. Allah!! He walked, smiling, to meet them!

(Everyone is looking at SAMI and GABE. Pause. RAYMOND finally speaks.)

RAYMOND: So he is a spy. We'll have to say so clearly, and wash our hands.

SAMI: *(Sharply)* No! He thought he could handle them!

RAYMOND: Sami, I believe, in this matter, your judgement is tainted.

SAMI: There's more to find out here, before we...

RAYMOND: I've got to act fast enough to minimize the damage!

TOMBO: *(On the board)* Headquarters in New York, Mr Raymond.

RAYMOND: *(Reaching for the phone)* I'll take it here.

(Rattle of a message being transmitted)

TOMBO: *(Reading off the teletype)* The Israelis are making an offer!

(The screens begin to fill with commentator reporting.)

SAMI: What good is it now?! What kind of a jackass move...?

RAYMOND: Politics, it's all politics.

VOICE-OVER: Defense Minister Yitzhak Rabin of Israel has offered a trade. All Israeli prisoners and Western hostages held by Shi'ite groups in Lebanon may be swapped for all the Shi'ite prisoners held by Israel, including Sheik Hajj.

(SAMI *stands like stone, watching.* TOMBO *tries to comfort him.*)

TOMBO: You know, sometimes they... Maybe the Hizballah waited. Maybe the deadline was a bluff.

SAMI: If they had, you think they'd buy this?! Hogie'd tell you—"when a polar bear's ass gets warm."

RAYMOND: *(On the phone)* We have evidence that it wasn't an abduction. Yes, that Hogan planned to meet his captors.

SAMI: *(Swinging around to take* GABE *by the shoulders)* Who's his contact, Gabe? We've got to do a trace.

GABE: *(Frightened)* I don't know. The Colonel's not a spy, he's....

SAMI: Tell me!

GABE: Nothing! The only name I remember is Todd.

SAMI: *(Gone pale, lets go of* GABE*)* What.

GABE: Todd. He just said he was in it for Todd.

(SAMI *backs to his desk, fumbles with the phone, and, checking a number, dials.*)

SAMI: Hello? Yes. Yes. What you should know is that it may be all over.

(*Onscreen,* LAUREL'*s picture is fading in.*)

SAMI: It may have been over even before the three P M deadline. We had reports...that he'd been killed accidentally, escaping, or being...interrogated. And we may never know what he was trying to do.

(*Behind her picture, we see* LAUREL *herself, talking on the phone.*)

LAUREL: *(Amplified)* I have to watch myself, you know, because I can just hear him saying "You big dumb broad, what are you bawling for?" So I just don't. Sami, you know what it is with him? He thinks he's the frigging Lone Ranger! Just gotta ride out and make that range safe for Americans. But he doesn't have a clue, not a clue! Listen, all I feel like is slugging him, for getting himself into this, and as soon as he gets back here, I'll...

SAMI: Laurel, there's something I need to know: What is it about...Todd?

LAUREL: Nothing! That's not it.

(LAUREL, *troubled, lowers the phone, and a light comes up on* HOGAN, *distant.*)

LAUREL: *(Impassioned)* I want you to talk to Todd!

HOGAN: But Laurel, if he's already signed the papers...

LAUREL: It makes sense that he'd do it to me, because I "lost" his father, but...

HOGAN: That's crap, Laurel. Take a deep breath. You sound hysterical.

LAUREL: And you just stand there, the big fat hero, while he worships! *(Quoting like a litany)* "Lieutenant Hogan, under enemy fire from three sides, in danger of being overrun, boldly advancing through 60 MM mortars, repeatedly exposing himself to..." *(Her voice cracks.)* You stand there on the mantel, he recites you by heart, and I don't want him locked up in that killing machine!

HOGAN: Todd may be trying to *find* his father, you know.

LAUREL: Well he won't find him in the Marines. He *died* there. You all die there. God, talking to you is like asking the devil to serve communion, but you've got to help me with him, Hogie, you've got to tell him not to enlist!

HOGAN: Laurel, we're not at war. Beirut is a peacekeeping post. He'll even be under orders *not* to fire.

(SAMI, still holding the phone, speaks urgently to RAYMOND, the others watching.)

SAMI: It's what I'm telling you. "Todd" was not a hostage. He was killed in the Marine barracks bombing.

RAYMOND: And Hogan knew it? Then he's mad.

SAMI: No, he just wanted it...to come out right.

(A deafening, blinding explosion fills the space. At its height we begin to hear HOGAN's scream.)

HOGAN: Tooooodd!!

(At the end of it we see only HOGAN kneeling opposite LAUREL, his hands extended to her. The rest of the space is in darkness.)

HOGAN: The one in the ceiling could have been Todd, but the hand was too big. So I kept looking, at each one, every piece, every face they uncovered, but I didn't find Todd, I couldn't find him, I...

(He breaks, sobbing, in her lap. LAUREL holds him, but stares straight ahead, turned to stone. The screens start to crackle with a transmission. The boards are dimly lit again.)

TOMBO: Something's coming in from Beirut.

(A form is coming into focus on the screen. HOGAN is gone. Reports come in, different voices meshing. SAMI covers his ears.)

VOICE-OVER: Outrageous. We demand immediate retaliatory action.

VOICE-OVER: Most practical—bombing or shelling...

VOICE-OVER: I'd like to think there are other ways....

TOMBO: Mary, Mother of God, save us.

(The image of a hanging man is now clear, panning up from bare feet to head, as he slowly twists.)

SAMI: *(Losing it)* There's no proof! There's no body! It's not him!

VOICE-OVER: Plans contemplate substantial amounts of "collateral damage," that is—civilian casualties.

RAYMOND: Sami! *(Grabs him)* Let it go! Take hold of yourself. You found him out. He instigated it all. He betrayed you. It was illegal, he's...

SAMI: No, can't you see? Past the muscle, the brass? He's a child. Just a child.

VOICE-OVER: It is impossible to make a definite determination on whether my husband is alive or dead. Give us proof!

SAMI: *(Lifts phone again)* You're seeing this, aren't you?

LAUREL: *(Spot-lit, at a distance, on the phone)* As far as gruesome goes, they couldn't do better. As far as if he's dead, I can't tell. All I can tell is...those are his toes.

(HOGAN becoming lit behind his hanged image, which is fading. He is lounging, at ease. The others are gone, except SAMI and LAUREL, whose light is dimming.)

VOICE-OVER: We can't blow up Lebanon to avenge the life of one American.

VOICE-OVER: There is no such thing as a "surgical raid" with five-hundred-pound bombs. It would feel good, but have no lasting impact.

LAUREL: *(Softly, almost humming)*
"And neither the angels in heaven above
nor the demons down under the sea
can ever dissever my soul from the soul
of the beautiful...."

(LAUREL's light is gone. HOGAN speaks intimately. SAMI listens.)

HOGAN: *(Easy)* You know that moment, Sami, very early, fuzzy gray, when you open your eyes and don't know who you are? I sometimes teeter there, wanting to start new, but if I shut my eyes again, it always happens: I find Todd.

(Music begins very low.)

HOGAN: And I promise her, next time we'll know why, there'll be a reason. Not because we don't know the first thing about who the hell people in what the hell country we've set our fat fanny down in!

But mostly I lie there in the fuzzy gray, you know how it is? Just part of that gray that's barely light at all, with nothing...attached to you, no memory of who is it you're supposed to be. That moment is so soft.

You think—did I have problems? Something I had to do? Someone I cared for? Then all the attachments return to make you a skin. You're the hero! You can get up. You forget it ever happened. It's just a moment...between dreaming you're someone else and knowing you aren't.

But I always wonder... Maybe that fuzzy gray moment was the real one If I can just get back to it, I'll figure things out differently. Hell, I'm no ace in this heroes business. I thought "work a quick deal, release a few Americans." Damned if I know what I was trying to... Seems like I'm leading a parade that turned the corner five blocks back! But I'm the hero. Aren't I?

So I think I *could* start new, floating there in the barely gray morning. I just need to...pull my skin on a little... differently.

(Music swells. Lights down to spot focus on HOGAN *and* SAMI. *Just before they go to black,* HOGAN *grins, salutes* SAMI, *as if to say "How about that?" And* SAMI *pulls on the blue beret.)*

END OF PLAY

www.ingramcontent.com/pod-product-compliance
Lightning Source LLC
Chambersburg PA
CBHW070802100426
42742CB00012B/2227